Reasons Bad Things Happen to Good People

Dave Earley

BARBOUR
PUBLISHING

The author is represented by literary agent Les Stobbe.

Published by Barbour Publishing, Inc., P.O. Box 719, Uhrichsville, Ohio 44683
www.barbourbooks.com

Our mission is to publish and distribute inspirational products offering exceptional value and biblical encouragement to the masses.

Printed in the United States of America.

Acknowledgments

Thanks to the great team of people who made this project a joy:

- Cathy, for being my traveling companion these past twenty-six years, for being such an encouragement, and for praying over, editing, and proofing every word.
- Luke, Andrew, and Daniel, for letting me tell some of your stories and for making me proud.
- Carol, for your amazing prayers and support.
- Sandy, for modeling perseverance in affliction.
- Steve, for being my favorite brother.
- Rod Bradley, Dave Jackson, Paul Coppel, and the other mighty men, for your prayers and encouragement.
- Terry Faulkenberry, Dave Martin, and Frank Carl, you have helped pastor us in our transition.
- Jim, Joan Angus, Dan Mitchell, Matt Chittum, Sujo John, and Saint Bert, for permitting me to tell your stories.
- Dave Wheeler, Rebecca Autry, Neil Grobler, Juan Dugan, David Brinkley, Becky Mahle, Julie Moore, Allen Anjo, and Chelsea Burkhalter, you are wonderful LCMT teammates.
- Elmer Towns, one day I might catch up with you.
- Paul Muckley, you are a joy to work with.
- Les Stobbe, for opening the door.
- Kelly Williams, for managing the in-house process, and Yolanda Chumney, for handling the typesetting.

Contents

Introduction: Why?. 7

1. The Reason No One Wants to Hear. 13

2. To Win an Unseen Victory. 21
   Job 1–2

3. To Expand Our Perspective of God 30
   Job 42:1–2

4. To Deepen Our Humility Before God 37
   Job 42:3

5. To Produce Greater Intimacy with God 43
   Job 42:5

6. To Prepare Us to Receive Far Greater Blessings 50
   Job 42

7. To Position Us for Higher Promotion. 57
   Genesis 50:20

8. To Prepare Us for the Miraculous. 64
   2 Chronicles 20

9. To Increase the Testimony of God 71
   Daniel 6

10. To Bring Us to Himself 79
    Acts 16

11. To Stretch Us for Greater Growth. 86
    ROMANS 5:3-4

12. To Remind Us That We Are Not Home Yet. 93
    ROMANS 8

13. To Shape Us More Like Jesus 100
    ROMANS 8:28-29

14. To Remind Us That We Are the Body of Christ. 108
    1 CORINTHIANS 12:12-14

15. To Equip Us for Further Ministry. 116
    2 CORINTHIANS 1:3-4

16. To Remove Our Self-Sufficiency 124
    2 CORINTHIANS 12:5-10

17. To Expand Our Evangelistic Efforts 131
    PHILIPPIANS 1:12-18

18. To Promote Us to Greater Glory. 138
    PHILIPPIANS 1:21; PSALM 116:15

19. To Give Us Further Instruction 144
    HEBREWS 12; PSALM 119:67, 71

20. To Call Us to Increased Prayer 152
    JAMES 1:5

21. To Refine Our Faith 160
    1 PETER 1:6-9

Final Thoughts 168

Introduction: Why?

"I haven't prayed in over a year. . . . Every time I try to pray,
I run headfirst into the same big, black wall: 'Why? Why did
God let this happen?' "

A senior at a Christian college, I was also the supervisor for a
dorm of young men. As the new school year began, we had joined
together with a girls' dorm for a coed hall meeting. You need to
understand that this was a fairly strict Christian college, so a coed
hall meeting was an exciting event. The guys saw it as a low-key
way to meet a lot of girls.

Afterward, all the guys were energized, especially the
freshmen. That is, all the guys were excited but one. His name
was Jim. He was in tears. I sat down next to him and asked,
"What's wrong?"

"Nothing," he said, trying to brush back the tears.

"Something's wrong," I said. "Tell me."

He began to choke on tears as he answered, "I prayed
tonight."

I was thinking, *Why is praying such a momentous event? This is
a* Christian *college, and we did have* everyone *say a prayer as part of
the program.* "So, we all did," I said.

"Yeah," he answered. "But that's the first time I've prayed in
over a year."

Jim went on to tell me his story. He had grown up in a strong
Christian family and had previously done well spiritually, praying
daily. He had come to a Christian college because he wanted to
become a pastor. Yet for the past year he had had no relationship
with God. He had no faith. He had nothing inside but empty,
hollow bitterness and doubt. Every time he tried to pray, one big
ugly word blocked it out. *Why? Why? Why?*

What had happened to turn him from God?

"My older sister is the best person I have ever known. She
loved God, was involved in everything at church. She never did
anything wrong," he explained.

"A little more than a year ago, some man got ahold of her. He beat her up and viciously raped her," Jim said through clenched teeth.

"She is the best person and the best Christian I know," he sobbed. Then he gulped on tears and looked at me. "Why did God allow this to happen? Why does God allow such terrible things to happen to good people?"

I have to admit I really did not know what to say. How would you answer his question? What do you say in the face of such pain?

Why *do* bad things happen to good people? It's a question we all ask. Every day in the newspaper we read the tragic tales of suffering, pain, and evil on planet Earth. Horribly bad things happen to very good people. Men with large families and women who are single moms lose their jobs. People get cancer. There are devastating floods and fires, hurricanes and tornadoes. Babies die or are born with crippling diseases. People are robbed, mugged, raped, abused, and murdered. In some parts of the world, Christians are tortured for their faith.

Why do such bad things happen to good people? It is a question that easily can become a great source of bitterness in our lives or in the lives of people we love.

Pain, suffering, and evil are relentless realities that will not go away until we are in heaven. Until then, what are we to do and think when bad things happen to good people?

This book is an attempt to answer Jim's question, "Why does God allow bad things to happen to good people?" It is a biblical study of potential benefits that come into our lives through suffering. It discusses twenty-one possible reasons bad things happen to good people. It is designed to be informative, inspiring, and encouraging. I hope reading it will nourish your faith so you can face the inevitable distress, the despair, the doubts, and the darkness that will confront your soul when you are hit with devastating hardship. But before we begin, let me frame our discussion by reminding you of several important truths.

1. *God is under no obligation to give us an explanation for suffering.*

Some say they don't want to believe in a god unless they can figure him out. But I have discovered that a god I can completely comprehend is no God at all. I am glad that the God I worship, the God I serve, the God I trust in the midst of suffering, pain, and evil is bigger than I can totally understand.

How big is our God? Our God is bigger than we can figure out and therefore big enough to see us through. He is a God who is beyond simple explanation. He is big enough for us to trust.

We don't want to hear it, but it's true. God is under no obligation to answer our questions. In this life, we may never see or fully understand why many things happen. That's what faith is about. It is trusting God *in the midst of*, trusting God *in spite of*, trusting God not only when we can see, but also *when we cannot see*.

2. *God has given us plenty of explanation if we will only look for it and accept it.*

The Bible gives many principles and examples to point us toward potentially productive reasons bad things happen to good people. The stories of Christians who have battled severe suffering show that God is able to produce much good from the bad we encounter. This book discusses many possible positive benefits that come into the life of the Christian through suffering.

3. *God can do more than one good thing through the bad things that happen to us.*

Have you ever had the delight of dropping a heavy rock into a still pond and seeing the many round ripples radiate out from the center? So it is with our episodes of suffering. They often drop like a weighty stone in a calm body of water and many good purposes may emanate from that point. We may not know the exact reason why bad things are happening to us, but we can know that good does come out—often many areas of good— radiating from one bad event.

4. *God knows what it is to suffer, and He knows how to help us in our suffering.*

Sometimes when we are hurting, we feel all alone and that, of all people, God has no idea what we are experiencing. This is a lie. Two thousand years ago, God stepped out of paradise so that He could experience our pain. He not only saw our suffering, but He tasted it, He wore it, He lived it, and He died as a result of it.

The ultimate and only pure picture of a bad thing happening to a good person is the cross. Jesus Christ was the only sinless person who ever lived. He is the Son of God and God the Son. Yet He experienced the ultimate in bad. Pain, suffering, sorrow, and evil resulting from sin filled the cup that Jesus drank in full measure.

> *The ultimate case of a bad thing happening to a truly good person was when the only truly good person, Jesus, was crucified for our sins.*

Are you struggling with emotional anguish? Many of the people Jesus had lovingly healed and fed called for His crucifixion. His friend betrayed Him, His best friend denied Him, and His followers abandoned Him. He was spit upon and mocked. Jesus knows about emotional pain.

Are you frustrated by injustice? The witnesses at the trial of Jesus lied about Him. The courts operated illegally to convict Him. Even the governor, after plainly stating, "I find no fault with this man," condemned Him to death.

Are you in physical pain? Remember that Jesus was beaten. He was whipped nearly to death with a whip designed to shred and rip the skin off His body. He experienced crucifixion—the most painful type of execution the Romans could imagine. Jesus died gasping for air, pulling against spikes in His wrists and feet, writhing for hours in front of a vicious crowd.

Is your battle against spiritual torment? The eternally innocent One, Jesus, had the filth of our sins dumped on Him. His own Father had to turn His back on His sin-covered Son. Darkness, torment, and hell filled the cup He drank down for us.

Imagine the excruciating agony of the heavenly Father, after an eternity in union with His Son, being forced to turn away at His Son's greatest point of need. Imagine having the power to remove all the pain from His Son but knowing that to do so would leave the world cursed by sin.

Does God know anything about pain? You have got to be kidding. On a much higher, deeper, broader level than we can possibly imagine, God experienced exactly what it is to have bad things happen to a good person. He knows what it is to suffer, and He knows how to help us in our suffering.

Are you in deep anguish? Battling bitterness? Staring at a thick wall of doubts and questions? Worn out by your pain?

You need God. Take your pain and turn it into prayer. Talk with God. Tell Him that you hurt. Tell Him you need encouragement.

He is there.

The Reason No One Wants to Hear

Maybe you are ready to dive into this book and read a collection of encouraging principles and uplifting stories of God bringing good to pass in the midst of very bad situations. I don't blame you. Suffering can be incredibly discouraging. When we hurt, we need every drop of encouragement we can get. So go for it. I suggest that you skip this chapter and go straight to chapter 2. You will find twenty soul-bracing chapters. Be stretched and see God being His awesome self and bringing plenty of positives for the negatives He allows His children to endure.

But if you are not in quite such a big hurry, I suggest that you slow down and read this chapter. It will become a big frame that is helpful in understanding the issue of why God allows bad things to happen to good people. But let me warn you: This chapter is the one no one wants to hear. Before we begin, it is important to understand that when we ask, "Why do bad things happen to good people?" there are assumptions behind why we even ask such a question.

The Assumptions behind the Question

When we ask, "Why would a good God allow bad things to happen to good people?" we ask this question based on three logical assumptions.

1. The world is full of suffering and evil.
2. God created the world.
3. Therefore, God is the one to blame!

1. "The world is full of suffering and evil." No doubt about that. Pain and suffering season the news every day of our lives. We live in a hurting world.

2. "God created the world." The Bible is very clear about God being the Creator of the universe (Genesis 1:1). This intricate universe had to come from somewhere. This effect had to be caused. Christians know that God is the ultimate Uncaused Cause who caused this universe to come into existence.

3. "Therefore, God is the one to blame!" We assume that if God is so good, then He would prevent bad things from happening. But He doesn't stop it. So, either God is not all that good or He is not powerful enough to stop evil from happening.

A Biblical Response to the Assumptions

The Bible gives one clear response to blaming God for suffering and evil: No, God is not the one to blame. Consider these five biblical truths:

1. *God created the world good.*

> *In the beginning God created the heavens and the earth. . . . God saw all that he had made, and it was very good.*
> GENESIS 1:1, 31

Yes, God created the world. But notice those last four words from Genesis 1:31: "it was very good." The word "good" used here means "admirable, suitable, pleasing, fully approved." When God created the world, there were no earthquakes, hurricanes, floods, droughts, sickness, murder, suicide, or crime. The world God made was very good. It was Paradise.

2. *God created people with the ability to choose.*

> *So God created man in his own image, in the image of*
> *God he created him; male and female he created them.*
> GENESIS 1:27

Being made in the image of God is what sets people apart from animals. Animals do not have a God-consciousness and cannot make moral choices. Humans can. God gave people the power to choose for several reasons.

First, choice is the essence of love. God let us choose because God loves us and wants us to choose to love Him back. Paul Little has written:

> But many ask, "Why didn't God make man so he couldn't sin?" To be sure, He could have, but let's remember that if He had done so we would no longer be human beings, we would be machines. How would you like to be married to a chatty doll? Every morning and every night you could pull the string and get the beautiful words, "I love you." There would never be any hot words, never any conflict, never anything said or done that would make you sad! But who would want that? There would never be any love, either. Love is voluntary. God could have made us like robots, but we would have ceased to be [human]. God apparently thought it worth the risk of creating us as we are.[1]

Second, choice is always a risk. When God let us choose, He let us take a risk. J. B. Phillips says, "Evil is inherent in the risky gift of free will."[2] He is right.

When our boys were younger, we gave them what we called "The Summer Challenge." We usually asked them to complete a project over the course of the summer, and if they did it, they would get a reward of their choice.

One of the first years we tried this, we challenged them to memorize and recite the eight verses called "the Beatitudes" (Matthew 5:3–12). They were to learn one a week. At the end of the summer, they could pick out any toy they wanted, up to a certain price, from Children's Palace. I turned them loose in the store and gave them thirty minutes to make their selection. My wife, Cathy, was certain they would choose something very educational. I wasn't so sure.

What do you think they selected? Educational games? No way. They chose instruments of destruction—toy rifles! We should have known. They are boys, and boys like guns. Giving them a choice was a risk.

3. *People chose evil.*

> *And the LORD God commanded the man, "You are free to eat from any tree in the garden; but you must not eat from the tree of the knowledge of good and evil, for when you eat of it you will surely die."*
> GENESIS 2:16–17

> *When the woman saw that the fruit of the tree was good for food and pleasing to the eye, and also desirable for gaining wisdom, she took some and ate it. She also gave some to her husband, who was with her, and he ate it.*
> GENESIS 3:6

God gave Adam and Eve a choice. What did they choose? They chose to disobey. They chose evil.

4. *Their choice brought evil into the world.*

> *Therefore, just as sin entered the world through one man, and death through sin, and in this way death*

came to all men, because all sinned.
ROMANS 5:12

Phillips writes, "Exercise of free choice in the direction of evil. . .is the basic reason for evil and suffering in the world."[3] When we think of blaming God for the evil in this world, we need to stop and remember that humans introduced evil into the world. Not God.

5. *Their choice has had lasting consequences.*

Since the Garden of Eden, the choice of Adam and Eve has had lasting implications. First, the world is no longer good.

> *For the creation was subjected to frustration, not by its own choice, but by the will of the one who subjected it, in hope that the creation itself will be liberated from its bondage to decay and brought into the glorious freedom of the children of God. We know that the whole creation has been groaning as in the pains of childbirth right up to the present time.*
> ROMANS 8:20–22

> *The Bible teaches that there is not always a one-to-one correspondence between sin and suffering. When we human beings told God to shove off, He partially honored our request. Nature began to revolt. The earth was cursed. Genetic breakdown and disease began. Pain and death became part of the human experience. The good creation was marred. We live in an unjust world. We are born into a world made chaotic and unfair by a humanity in revolt against its Creator.[4]*

Why are there earthquakes? The answer is that we live in a sin-cursed world that has subterranean faults. Why did you get sick? The answer is because we live in a world with germs. We no longer live in Paradise. The world now is abnormal. The world is no longer good. It is flawed, as is everything in it, including us.

People are no longer "good." Romans 3:10 says, "There is no one righteous, not even one." We need to remember that the blame for the majority of human evil and suffering lies at the feet of human irresponsibility.

> *How can you blame God for starving babies in Ethiopia when the best-selling books in the United States are on dieting, on how to take the extra fat off? It is not God's fault people are starving today. The earth produces enough right now to give every person 3,000 calories a day. The problem is that some of us hoard so others go to bed hungry. It is a cop-out to blame God for human irresponsibility. If a person gets drunk, drives his car across the median, and sends your friend to an early grave, will you blame God? Do you blame God for Hitler's seven million murders? That would be escapism. The vast majority of human evil and suffering is the direct result of human irresponsibility.[5]*

Drunker Than Skunks

The world is no longer good, and people are not perfectly good. I'm not sure I believed that until I had kids. I knew I was not good, but it seemed that there had to be some purely good people out there. Then we had kids. Cathy and I have three amazing sons, but I have found that I didn't have to go out of my way to teach them how to be *bad*. They have a way of picking that up on their own. I had to go out of my way to teach them to be *good*.

When my sons were much younger, we watched an old movie together, *The Adventures of Huck Finn*. Then I put them in the bathtub, attempting to give them a bath. The phone rang, so I left the bathroom for just a minute or two. Soon I heard a wild ruckus coming from the bathroom. I rushed in to see them laughing and acting crazy.

I put my hands on my hips and did my best "intimidating dad" routine, saying, "What is wrong with you boys?"

Four-year-old Daniel piped up, "We're drunk."

"Drunker than skunks," two-year-old Andrew added merrily.

"What?" I said, shocked by their response. "You guys have never seen any drunk people. Where did you get this idea?"

Daniel looked at me proudly and replied, "Huck Finn's dad. He was drunk."

"Drunker than a skunk," Andrew chimed in.

I could not believe it. We had watched a clean, classic, two-hour movie, and what had they learned? How to get drunk!

The next night it was Luke's turn. Luke was a cooperative, well-behaved toddler. He was easygoing, generally quick to please and obey. When he was about eighteen months old, we had pizza for supper. We tried to feed him a piece, but a defiant look rose in his eye. He did not want *this* piece; he had to have *that* piece. Then he did not want *that* piece; he had to have *another* piece. He did not want *those* pieces; he had to have *my* piece.

Exasperated, Cathy looked at me and said, "What's wrong with him?"

Then I had an epiphany.

I looked at her and said, "Well, theologically speaking. . .he's a sinner."

So were Adam and Eve. So are you and I. God gave us the ability to choose between right and wrong. We sometimes choose wrong. We have proven that if it had been us in the Garden of Eden, we would have made the same choice. We are sinners by nature.

I once had a guy come up to me in the grocery store. He was eager to tell me a big, dark secret. "Pastor, there's something you need to know about your church," he said.

"Really, what's that?" I asked.

"I hate to break it to you, but you have some *sinners* going to your church."

"What!" I looked at him and said, "Sir, if there were no *sinners* in my church, there would be no *people* in my church."

Why?

We ask, "Why do bad things happen to good people?" But if we really want to be honest, we have to reword the question. Considering this issue, we can conclude that instead of asking why so many bad things happen to good people, we should ask ourselves why so many good things happen to bad people.

Instead of being bitter over the hardships we face, we must be thankful for all the blessings we enjoy. We can anticipate the perfect, pain-free life we will enjoy in heaven. We also need to learn that our God produces many good things from the bad.

Notes

1. Paul Little, *Know Why You Believe* (Downers Grove, IL: InterVarsity, 1988), 132.
2. J. B. Phillips, *God Our Contemporary* (New York: Macmillan, 1960), 88.
3. Ibid.
4. Cliffe Knechtle, *Give Me an Answer That Satisfies My Heart and Mind* (Downers Grove, IL: InterVarsity, 1986), 54.
5. Knechtle, *Give Me an Answer*, 52.

To Win an Unseen Victory
JOB 1-2

The fact that you are reading this book tells me that, at least at some level, you are confronting adversity and the inevitable questions evoked by suffering. Maybe someone you love has had his or her world racked by excruciating pain. Possibly you are the one standing toe to toe with untold agony. Overrun by adversity and ransacked by sorrow, answers are sought and encouragement is required. You are not alone on the road of suffering. Although often very lonely, it is heavily traveled and has been since the earliest days of history. Although your situation seems unique and extreme, rest assured, others have also drunk deeply from the cup of sorrow. One man's massive misery makes even my most severe seasons of suffering seem almost tame and tiny. He is the poster boy of pain. His name is Job.

Life Was Very, Very Good

> Job was. . .honest inside and out, a man of his word,
> who was totally devoted to God and hated evil with
> a passion. He had seven sons and three daughters. He
> was also very wealthy—seven thousand head of sheep,
> three thousand camels, five hundred teams of oxen, five
> hundred donkeys, and a huge staff of servants—the
> most influential man in all the East!
> JOB 1:1–3 THE MESSAGE

In the thumbnail sketch drawn by those three verses, we know several important facts about Job's life. First, he was a good man. In fact, he was about as good a man as could be found.

Second, he was a family man who enjoyed his seven sons and three daughters. Elsewhere in Job chapter 1, we find that he regularly prayed for his children (v. 5).

Third, Job had it made! One of the richest, most influential men in his part of the world, he had huge flocks and herds, and a large staff to care for them.

The envy of all, Job could truly look around and say, "Life is good!"

Life Turned Very, Very Bad

> While Job's children were having one of their parties at the home of the oldest son, a messenger came to Job and said, "The oxen were plowing and the donkeys grazing in the field next to us when Sabeans attacked. They stole the animals and killed the field hands. I'm the only one to get out alive and tell you what happened."
>
> While he was still talking, another messenger arrived and said, "Bolts of lightning struck the sheep and the shepherds and fried them—burned them to a crisp. I'm the only one to get out alive and tell you what happened."
>
> While he was still talking, another messenger arrived and said, "Chaldeans coming from three directions raided the camels and massacred the camel drivers. I'm the only one to get out alive and tell you what happened."
>
> While he was still talking, another messenger arrived and said, "Your children were having a party at the home of the oldest brother when a tornado swept in off the desert and struck the house. It

> *collapsed on the young people and they died. I'm the*
> *only one to get out alive and tell you what happened."*
> JOB 1:13–19 THE MESSAGE

I can't possibly imagine! In one day, one single day, every nightmare and every unspoken fear that had ever sneaked like a thief into the corners of Job's mind exploded into reality and hit him like a train wreck. With no warning, Job's family and fortune were swept away in a landslide of loss. In one day, his job, his employees, his property, his income, his retirement, and his lifework were all totally, terrifyingly taken away. All he had worked for, all he had dreamed of, all he had owned was gone.

In one day, the precious ones who proudly bore his image and carried his name, the ones he had joyfully watched take their very first steps, the ones he diligently prayed for, were cruelly killed, their promising lives prematurely snuffed out. I can't imagine losing one child, but ten! All at the same time! All gone! Oh, the agony!

Numb? Crushed? Flattened? What words can possibly describe what he must have felt? Job's mountainous good fortune had suddenly become a gaping crater of what used to be. His very, very good life had turned violently and vilely bad.

Why would a good God possibly allow one of His most faithful servants to suffer so unjustly? What was God thinking? Why didn't He protect Job? Why did He allow it to happen?

The Scene behind the Scenes

God and Satan are locked in a cosmic battle for loyalty and allegiance, and often, we are the battleground. What Job was not able to see was that his sorrow was birthed out of an intriguing conversation Satan had with God.

> GOD *said to Satan, "Have you noticed my friend Job?*
> *There's no one quite like him—honest and true to his*

word, totally devoted to God and hating evil."

Satan retorted, "So do you think Job does all that out of the sheer goodness of his heart? Why, no one ever had it so good! You pamper him like a pet, make sure nothing bad ever happens to him or his family or his possessions, bless everything he does—he can't lose!

"But what do you think would happen if you reached down and took away everything that is his? He'd curse you right to your face, that's what."

GOD replied, "We'll see. Go ahead—do what you want with all that is his. Just don't hurt him." Then Satan left the presence of GOD.

JOB 1:8–12 THE MESSAGE

As we have already discussed, Satan left God and proceeded to have Job's livestock, his servants, and his children killed. Yet this situation extended far beyond Job, his animals, his employees, or his children. The unjust, unprovoked suffering of one single man standing alone in the entire universe struck at the very heart of the greatest conflict in the complete scope of human history. That is a stunning reality.

The question of evil and suffering on planet Earth must be understood as a spiritual battleground. There is more at stake than the comfort or heartache of a single sufferer. Monumental issues may be at stake. Massive questions may be hanging on the response of a lone individual.

"Will a man continue to loyally follow God even when he is overwhelmed by unexpected, unprovoked, inexplicable evil?"

"Is God worth it?"

"Does He merit such loyalty?"

Satan knew that no one with his or her eyes wide open to the facts would fully follow him if he did not bribe that person with forbidden powers and pleasures. He knew that his intrinsic nature does not merit such loyalty. He is not worth it. Out of blind arrogance and jealousy, he refused to believe that God is worth such allegiance. So he staged a high-stakes chess game with God, and poor Job served as the pawn. Surprisingly, God played along.

Job's Response

So, how did Job respond when struck by a tsunami of suffering? Did Job's reaction prove Satan to be right or God to be worthy? After getting the last report that his children had all been killed in a tornado, note carefully Job's next step.

> *Job got to his feet, ripped his robe, shaved his head,*
> *then fell to the ground and worshiped: Naked I came*
> *from my mother's womb, naked I'll return to the*
> *womb of the earth. GOD gives, GOD takes. God's name*
> *be ever blessed.*
> *Not once through all this did Job sin; not once did*
> *he blame God.*
> JOB 1:20–22 THE MESSAGE

Yeah, Job! Crushed, broken, aching, and numb, Job still worshipped God. Job's response to suffering proved that he believed God to be worthy of worship even when everything was taken away and life turned horribly, terribly ugly. God won! Satan lost! Yeah, God!

Bad Turned Worse

Before Job had a chance to catch his breath or get his feet back under him, before his aching heart could begin to heal, bad turned worse—much, much worse.

> *Satan. . .struck Job with terrible sores. Job was ulcers*
> *and scabs from head to foot. They itched and oozed so*
> *badly that he took a piece of broken pottery to scrape*

> *himself, then went and sat on a trash heap, among the*
> *ashes.*
> JOB 2:7–8 THE MESSAGE

If the inner agony caused by loss of family and fortune was not enough, now Job had the outer anguish of boils. Why would a good God possibly allow one of His most faithful servants to suffer so unjustly? What was God thinking? Why didn't He protect Job? Why did He allow it to happen?

The Scene behind the Scenes, Part 2

Satan did not give up easily. His ability to "take a lickin' and keep on tickin' " is impressive. After Job initially responded to his loss by worshipping God anyway, Satan pulled himself off the mat to fight round two.

> *Then GOD said to Satan, "Have you noticed my friend*
> *Job? There's no one quite like him, is there—honest*
> *and true to his word, totally devoted to God and*
> *hating evil? He still has a firm grip on his integrity!*
> *You tried to trick me into destroying him, but it didn't*
> *work."*
> *Satan answered, "A human would do anything*
> *to save his life. But what do you think would happen*
> *if you reached down and took away his health? He'd*
> *curse you to your face, that's what."*
> *GOD said, "All right. Go ahead—you can do*
> *what you like with him. But mind you, don't kill*
> *him."*
> JOB 2:3–6 THE MESSAGE

Satan again challenged God's integrity by attacking Job's. He said that even if Job had not given in and given up on God after losing everything, Job would certainly throw in the towel if God allowed Satan to attack his health.

Ever secure in the knowledge of His incredible worth, and confident in the depth of Job's character and loyalty, God said, "Yes." So, as we read earlier, Satan raced out and coated Job with ugly, aching, pus-oozing boils.

Job's Response, Part 2

> *His wife said, "Still holding on to your precious integrity, are you? Curse God and be done with it!"*
> *He told her, "You're talking like an empty-headed fool. We take the good days from God—why not also the bad days?"*
> *Not once through all this did Job sin. He said nothing against God.*
> Job 2:9–10 the message

Yeah, Job. . .again! Anguish piled upon anguish, sorrow heaped upon sorrow, grief loaded upon grief, yet Job still worshipped God. Job's response to suffering proved that he believed God to be worthy of worship even when suffering the zenith of emotional *and* physical pain. God won again! Satan lost again! Yeah, God—again!

A Reason Bad Things Happen to Good People

Let me stretch your thinking for just a few moments. This is an amazing thought. Maybe some of our suffering has little or nothing to do with us and everything to do with God's plan to silence Satan's pride, to shut Satan's mouth. Satan wants to be worshipped like God, but he knows he is not worth it. If his followers were put in the same position in which Job was placed, they would turn on him very quickly.

Yet, when one of God's followers, in this case Job, lost everything, he refused to turn. God was worth it. And Satan was shut up.

There are forty more chapters in the book of Job, and do you know how many times Satan is mentioned after chapter 2? None, nada, zero, zip! Why? Satan is no longer mentioned because Satan was thoroughly silenced by the stunning worthiness of God as seen in the extraordinary integrity of Job. He was shut out, soundly defeated. God had won and Satan had lost, so he slunk off in embarrassed silence.

I love it!

Wow! One little human who suffered so triumphantly had the power to shut the mouth of the prince of darkness! He did not bind the enemy with some well-worded prayer. He did not call down fire from heaven to burn up the enemy. He just remained loyal to God even though bad things were crashing in all around him. He was faithful in spite of a heart broken by grief and a body broken by pain. Job did not realize it at the time, but he was winning an unseen victory. Wow!

Friend, maybe the bad things that are happening to you right now really don't have to do with you so much as with the titanic struggle of the universe. Maybe the entire kingdom of darkness and the entire kingdom of God are watching to see how you handle your pain, in order to know if your life proves that God is truly worthy.

Edith Schaeffer, in her book *Affliction*, takes this concept to a higher level when she proposes that this scenario has been reenacted over and over throughout history. She imagines a conversation similar to one in which Satan says to God, "Okay, so Job kept trusting You, but what if a woman had five sons die in the war? She would not continue trusting You." God replies, "Look at Mrs. So and So, whose five sons died in the Civil War and she kept trusting Me." Satan comes back the next day and says, "Okay, so she trusted You, but what if a man lost his wife and baby in a fire? He would not continue trusting You." God replies, "Well, Joe So and So lost his wife and baby in a fire and he kept on trusting Me."[1]

The idea is that by the time Jesus comes and ends history as we know it, every conceivable type of affliction will have been courageously faced by one of us making Satan's defeat and silence complete. His big mouth will be permanently shut and he will have to get on his knees and declare that Jesus is Lord (Philippians 2:9–11).

Schaeffer writes, "There is titanic meaning and purpose in our individual afflictions, since the particular one Satan is hitting us with today has not been lived through before at any time in history—nor will it be again."[2] Each of us faces unique and individual sets of suffering. Therefore, our afflictions and responses truly matter to God, and our response may impact history!

> *This to me is the fabulous "discovery of all discoveries"—that God is so fair that He enables us each to have the opportunity to have outstanding things to do in His total history of victory through the ages. . . . We cannot know which [affliction] will turn out to be the most important moment in our lives. Its arrival won't be announced with a blast of silver horns or blare of an orchestra's full crescendo. Our most important moment can come when no one but God and Satan are aware of it, when our response to the Lord is one which at once wins a battle [against our unseen foe].[3]*

Why?

So why do bad things happen to good people? What good can come from the bad? It could be that there is an unseen victory to be won. Maybe we don't realize it now, but we may be players in an unseen battle. Our response to suffering may give God greater glory and get Satan to shut up.

Wow!

Notes

1. Edith Schaeffer, *Affliction* (Old Tappan, NJ: Revell, 1978), 76.
2. Ibid., 77.
3. Ibid., 78–79.

3

To Expand Our Perspective of God
Job 42:1–2

August 18, 1991, is a day I will never forget. I woke up that morning with a raging case of the flu that never quite went away. I dropped from 140 pounds to 122 pounds in three weeks. There was a persistent pain in my joints and muscles that grew steadily more intense through the day. Mysteriously, the slightest bit of cold air made it all the worse. My head felt like it was trapped in a vise as I carried around a sharp headache that refused to go away. Suddenly, I was allergic to all sorts of things. A whiff of grass, perfume, leaves, pets, or any of a number of other things would make my eyes water, throat tighten, and head ache even more.

Frustratingly, my cognitive capacities would short-circuit. I could see words in my head but found myself incapable of getting them smoothly out of my mouth—not a good thing when you are a pastor. I could not sleep for more than a few hours at a time. Without fail, about five o'clock every night, I would get a terrible sore throat and an ugly, dark cloud of despair would fill my soul.

But the greatest aggravation was the incredible crushing fatigue that weighed me down as if I were encased in cement and trying to run underwater. Day after day after day, I woke up aching and tired and grew more exhausted as the day wore on. Night after night, I'd lie in bed and have to concentrate on mustering all of my strength just so I could turn over by myself. I had been an athlete in college, yet now I had days when the big adventure was trying to crawl down the hall to the bathroom by myself.

Making it worse was the fact that my three sons were all under the age of five. My little boys had a hard time understanding why I couldn't get off the couch to play with them like I used to or why I could not go out to make a snowman.

Beyond that, my church was going through a difficult period of transition. As the senior pastor, it was important that I invest additional energy in helping navigate the church through the challenging waters it faced. Yet I did not have any extra energy.

Topping it all off was the awful guilt. With three little boys, my wife really needed me to help out around the house and with the children. Yet I was overwhelmed with trying to take care of myself and trying to continue to lead a church. It was horrible to see how my exhaustion was wearing her out.

After months of seeing multiple doctors and specialists, I was eventually diagnosed with chronic fatigue immune deficiency syndrome. (My male ego was bruised to find that it is an illness contracted most frequently by overachieving females.) CFIDS, at that time, was an illness few people understood.

It was awful being a POW to my pain and fatigue. I had always been such a driven, goal-oriented person, and now I was unable to pursue any goal beyond daily survival.

But more than anything, I was deeply disappointed in God. The only response He gave was silence—blank, empty, hollow, deafening silence. Day after day I asked for deliverance, yet nothing happened. Then I began to ask for at least some sort of explanation or, at the very minimum, a time frame for my agony.

I read and reread the book of Job, searching for a time frame. How long did Job suffer? I even asked some of the best Bible scholars in the country that question, and they all had the same infuriating answer: "The Bible does not say."

Day after day, week after week, month after month, God said nothing. My illness continued and months stretched into years, yet God refused to answer me.

I was determined to get His attention, so I prayed diligently for an hour a day. I fasted. Yet God was still silent.

It felt like He had abandoned me, and I had no idea why. I was not living in sin. I was serving Him diligently.

Why would He allow this to happen?

Why did He not intervene?

Why didn't He at least give me some explanation?

Why wouldn't He tell me when it would end?

Yet, God remained silent.[1]

No Explanation Given

Although my suffering was small compared to Job's, it was just as real. Therefore, I think I can understand some of the frustration Job felt as he looked up from the devastation that had been his life and cried out to God for an explanation yet heard nothing from God. Through much of his story, Job wanted a chance to defend his cause before God and receive some type of clarification as to why he was forced to suffer such severe sorrow. Yet chapter after chapter, all Job received from God was the deafening cacophony of absolute silence. Note the keen note of frustration in his voice.

> *"If I have sinned, what have I done to you, O watcher of men? Why have you made me your target? Have I become a burden to you?"*
> JOB 7:20

> *"Though one wished to dispute with him, he could not answer him one time out of a thousand."*
> JOB 9:3

> *"Even if I summoned him and he responded, I do not believe he would give me a hearing."*
> JOB 9:16

> *"He is not a man like me that I might answer him,*
> *that we might confront each other in court. If only*
> *there were someone to arbitrate between us, to lay his*
> *hand upon us both."*
> Job 9:32–33

> *"I will say to God: Do not condemn me, but tell me*
> *what charges you have against me."*
> Job 10:2

> *"I desire to speak to the Almighty and to argue my case*
> *with God."*
> Job 13:3

As you read the book of Job, you find that for 36 chapters (chapters 3–38), Job honestly bemoaned his fate and defended himself against the criticisms of his self-righteous friends. For 36 chapters, he sought God for an explanation. For 36 chapters, possibly spanning months or even longer, God did not answer.

No Explanation Needed

Finally, in chapter 38, God miraculously stepped to the stage. The Lord honored Job by addressing him from out of a storm. But instead of giving Job answers, the Lord took Job on a tour of creation. Instead of answering Job's questions, the Lord grilled Job with a flurry of rhetorical questions revealing the immense gulf between God, the infinite Creator, and Job, the insignificant creation. The entire scene is designed to put the matter of Job's suffering and loss into a much bigger perspective.

No Explanation Necessary

Through his loss and grief, Job came to a much deeper realization of the immense and sovereign personhood of God.

> *Then Job replied to the LORD: "I know that you can do*
> *all things; no plan of yours can be thwarted."*
> JOB 42:1–2

Note the conviction in Job's voice. He now "knew" that God can do all things. He understood that God is, well, God, and is answerable to no one. No one can be higher than the Highest or mightier than the Almighty. The Lord is so exceedingly before, above, and beyond humanity that it is ridiculous to think we could possibly pull Him down to our level by demanding answers, reasons, and explanations. God does not have to explain Himself to us or anyone else. He owes us no answers. He can and will do what He deems right. Job observed:

> *"In his hand is the life of every creature and the breath*
> *of all mankind. . . . To God belong wisdom and power;*
> *counsel and understanding are his. What he tears down*
> *cannot be rebuilt; the man he imprisons cannot be*
> *released. If he holds back the waters, there is drought;*
> *if he lets them loose, they devastate the land. To him*
> *belong strength and victory; both deceived and deceiver*
> *are his. . . . He makes nations great, and destroys them;*
> *he enlarges nations, and disperses them."*
> JOB 12:10, 13–16, 23

God may be doing things that are bigger than we can imagine and, as in the case of Job, our suffering may be part of something much bigger than we. What He is up to may be beyond the realm of our comprehension (Isaiah 55:8). Job saw that God is the absolute ruler of all creation. He did not know everything about God, but he knew enough to trust God in the things he did not know.

Possessing a bigger, more accurate view of God is a very valuable gift. A. W. Tozer writes, "What comes to mind when we think of God is the most important thing about us."[2]

What would be the best thing you or I could ever possess? The best answer is "God," as every good and perfect gift comes from Him and is found in Him. When it comes to God, what would be the best thing you or I could obtain? The answer is "an accurate view of the immense size of our infinite God." To our detriment, we too easily forget how infinitely big, intelligent, powerful, and good is our God. As Tozer notes,

> *The [one] who comes to a right belief about God is relieved of ten thousand temporal problems, for he sees at once that these have to do with matters which at the most cannot concern him for very long.*[3]

A Bigger Perspective of God

Why did God allow Job to suffer? Why did God initially respond to Job with thunderous silence? Why did God give Job a lesson in His power instead of an answer to Job's questions?

One of the good things that may come from bad things is a sense of clearer, bigger perspective. Ultimately we need God far more than we need explanations. Sometimes we need to get a larger view of God and of life.

The Terrible, Wonderful Fire

There is a Norwegian folktale about a fisherman who, with his two sons, went out on their daily fishing run. Their catch was good, but by midafternoon a sudden and severe storm blotted out the shoreline, leaving the men groping for the slightest sight of home. Meanwhile, a ferocious fire broke out in the kitchen of their home. Before it could be extinguished, it had destroyed everything.

Finally, the sons and their father were able to row to shore. The man's wife was awaiting him with the tragic news of the fire.

"Karl," she sobbed, "a terrible fire has destroyed everything.

We have nothing left."

Yet he was unfazed.

"Didn't you hear me?" she pleaded. "The house is gone."

"Yes, I heard you," he said calmly.

"How can you be so calm?" she pleaded.

"You don't understand. A few hours ago we were completely lost at sea. I was sure we would perish." He continued, "Then something happened. I saw a strange golden glow. It grew larger and larger. We decided to steer toward that light."

Then grabbing her shoulders and looking into her eyes, he said, "Don't you see? The terrible fire that destroyed our house was the wonderful fire that saved our lives. God had it under control. God is a big God."

Sometimes houses and health seem to be so very important, but suffering has a way of adjusting our perspective—especially our view of God.

Why?

Why did God allow Job to suffer? Why did God initially respond to Job with thunderous silence? Why did God give Job a lesson in His power instead of an answer to Job's questions? One of the many good things that can come from very bad things is a clearer, bigger perspective. More important than knowing exactly why we are suffering is the knowledge gained of God through our suffering. More significant than receiving an explanation for our pain is embracing a bigger view of God through our pain.

Allow your questions, doubts, and pain to press you closer to God than ever before.

Notes

1. This story is adapted from Dave Earley, *Prayer Odyssey* (Shippensburg, PA: Destiny-Image Publishers, 2001), 167–68, and used by permission.
2. A. W. Tozer, *The Knowledge of the Holy* (New York: Harper and Row, 1961), 9.
3. Ibid., 10.

To Deepen Our Humility Before God

JOB 42:3

Peeling the Onion

The last few months of my dad's life were a tough time for both of us. He had been a very healthy, capable, sharp, bright, lively, witty, successful businessman deep into his seventies. Even in the years after he retired, he was independent in every way. But weakened by the ravages of the final stages of bone cancer, he became dependent on people and needed help.

He could not drive, do his laundry, or shop for his groceries. He was too weak to even write out checks to pay his bills. He needed help getting to the bathroom. He was unable to bathe or dress himself.

His transition to dependence was extremely hard on both of us. He had always been so abundantly capable that it was humiliating to need the help of his son. I was the one who had always depended on him. He was a rock, a foundation, the one person I could always trust. But roles were eerily reversed. The father had become the child and the child the parent, and neither of us liked it.

One day as he lay in bed, he had an unexpected bowel movement, and I was the only one around to clean it up. The thought of me cleaning him up made us both very tense, uncomfortable, and embarrassed. We avoided making eye contact. We both wanted to get it cleaned up and to move on as quickly as possible. But with an emaciated eighty-two-year-old man and an inexperienced forty-five-year-old son, cleaning up the mess was not quick or easy. Uncharacteristically, he barked at me, and I barked back. He did not want to be seen like this, and neither did I.

After the ordeal was over and he was safely back in bed, in clean clothes, lying on clean sheets, I noticed tears filling his eyes. At least that is what I thought I saw. It was hard to be sure because I was looking out of my own tear-filled eyes. I wish I could write that he cracked a joke and we both broke into a laugh, but I can't. His cancer was breaking us both. It was revealing levels of pride neither of us had known existed. The whole process was incredibly hard. Pride is a rock that is uneasily broken.

Someone once described the process of true examination as peeling an onion, in that the exposure of each new layer brings a fresh set of tears. One of the extremely good benefits of suffering is that it uncovers and unwraps layers of inner pride, independence, arrogance, self-will, self-centeredness, and selfishness that would be exposed no other way. This exposure is very painful but also essential. Through hopeless brokenness comes the amazingly beautiful and liberating virtue called humility.

He Humbled Himself

Apart from selfless love, no virtue is more Christian than humility. Everything Jesus accomplished for us as the Son of God flowed from His humility. In the great passage theologians refer to as "the kenosis of the Christ," the apostle Paul shows us the deep extent and marvelous fruit of the humility of Jesus.

> *Think of yourselves the way Christ Jesus thought of himself. He had equal status with God but didn't think so much of himself that he had to cling to the advantages of that status no matter what. Not at all. When the time came, he set aside the privileges of deity and took on the status of a slave, became* human! *Having become human, he stayed human.* It was an

> incredibly humbling process. *He didn't claim special
> privileges. Instead, he lived a selfless, obedient life and
> then died a selfless, obedient death—and the worst kind
> of death at that: a crucifixion.*
>
> *Because of that obedience, God lifted him high
> and honored him far beyond anyone or anything, ever,
> so that all created beings in heaven and on earth—
> even those long ago dead and buried—will bow in
> worship before this Jesus Christ, and call out in praise
> that he is the Master of all, to the glorious honor of
> God the Father.*
>
> PHILIPPIANS 2:5–11 THE MESSAGE (emphasis added)

"It was an incredibly humbling process." I guess so! Think about it. Jesus willingly let go of more than we can ever possibly imagine. No one ever experienced the level of humility Jesus willingly endured. He endured the humility of no longer having free access to infinite riches, but instead became totally dependent on others. Jesus experienced what it means to leave a glorious dwelling in a breathtakingly beautiful place and take up residence in a borrowed barn. He underwent the frustration of no longer being able to walk or feed Himself, because long ago, He became a helpless baby.

Instead of being treated as God, He became a member of a despised nation of slaves. No longer served by legions of angels, He instead became the servant of all. Rather than closely associating with mighty angels, His new companions became the hurting, the helpless, and the broken. Instead of being worshipped as God, He was called a bastard, a liar, and a lunatic. Beyond that, He was beaten, spit upon, scourged, and executed.

Because Jesus humbled Himself, justice was treated unjustly. Love was betrayed, abandoned, and rejected. Truth was mocked.

King became slave. God became man. The Ancient of Days became infant.

Jesus knows humility.

I do not know what flavor of humility it is that adversity is forcing down your throat, but I do know that Jesus has already drunk at the same well. In every conceivable way a man could be humbled, Jesus Christ was humbled. Because of it, we call Him Lord, Master of all, and King of kings.

Nothing makes us more like Jesus than pure humility. Nothing is as honored by God as true humility.

A Humbled Man

Job was the richest, most highly esteemed man around—until adversity hit. His entire life's work was gone in a day. His income, job, career, and retirement were wiped out in a few dreadful hours. His prestige was removed. Instead of being honored by those he had never even met, he was mocked by strangers. Instead of being envied and feared, he was scorned.

Job believed he could endure all of that if only God would give him an audience, if only he could defend himself before the Almighty. Yet, when it finally happened, it did not turn out as he hoped. Instead of impressing God with the justice of his cause, Job was left dumbfounded by the immense power and sovereign authority of the Creator and God of the universe. Job felt stupid for even imagining that he could somehow straighten God out and show Him a thing or two.

Nevertheless, good came from the bad.

One sweet fruit of Job's heinous suffering was the flower of deeper humility blooming more brightly in his life. His testimony is that the experience left him a changed man. Instead of being the one with all the answers, he had nothing much to say.

> *"You asked, 'Who is this that obscures my counsel without knowledge?' Surely I spoke of things I did not understand, things too wonderful for me to know."*
> JOB 42:3

Adversity has a way of reminding us that we are not the

center of the universe. Pain has the power to point out our insufficiency. It reminds us, often brutally, of our naked insecurity, broken vulnerability, often overlooked mortality, and immense dependency. It forces us to depend on others and turn to God. When suffering has thrown us flat on our back and we have nowhere to look but up, it is only then that we truly see God.

Rudy

I am a sucker for underdog, feel-good movies. One of my favorites is *Rudy*, the story of the too short, too slow, too dumb kid who longed to play big-time football at Notre Dame University. After doing his all-out best and receiving yet another severe setback, he went to see his priest. The old man gave him a wonderful word of advice when he said, "After a lifetime of theological studies, I have discovered but two indisputable truths—there is a God and I am not He."

We are not God. Yet we are upset when life does not come under our control and play out as we planned. Suffering is never in our plans, and facing it humbles us. Humility is an accurate assessment of oneself and of God. It is only through setbacks, suffering, and sorrows that we really understand who we are, who we aren't, and even more important, who He really is. This sense of deeper humility is one of the great benefits of affliction.

Humility Is a Magnet

> *For this is what the high and lofty One says—he who lives forever, whose name is holy: "I live in a high and holy place, but also with him who is contrite and lowly in spirit, to revive the spirit of the lowly and to revive the heart of the contrite."*
> ISAIAH 57:15

This verse is an amazing promise. The Lord, who is above and beyond anyone and all else, pledges to be with the hurting, helpless, hopeless, and humble. When difficulties knock us down, God will reach down and pick us up. When trouble draws near, God draws nearer. True heartbroken humility is like a magnet that attracts the God who is hopelessly in love with the hopeless.

God Is No Fan of Self-Sufficient Pride

> *"God opposes the proud but gives grace to the humble."*
> JAMES 4:6

> *"For whoever exalts himself will be humbled, and whoever humbles himself will be exalted."*
> MATTHEW 23:12

> All of you, clothe yourselves with humility toward one another, because, *"God opposes the proud but gives grace to the humble."*
> 1 PETER 5:5

God opposes the proud. He stiff-arms the self-sufficient. God is nauseated by conceit and sickened by smugness. After all, He is God. Nothing we do, say, think, have, or are can impress Him. He made us from dust. He has seen it all, owns it all, and can do it all. In the light of who He is, human pride, arrogance, and boasting are ridiculous and odious. He simply stiff-arms them out of His way, or He graciously allows them to be broken.

Because affliction deepens our humility, it draws us nearer to God than we would be otherwise. This is a marvelous blessing that comes through buffeting.

Why?

So why does a good God allow bad things to happen to good people? Often it is to bring us to a deeper level of humility. Humility is a virtue that opens the door to many true blessings and is a place where God can meet us. Allow the suffering you are experiencing to produce a deeper level of humility in your life.

To Produce Greater Intimacy with God

JOB 42:5

When someone else is hurting, we wrestle with the theoretic "problem of evil." We ask, "Why does a good God allow bad things happen to good people?" However, when we are the one who is suffering, the question often changes. We no longer are as interested in a philosophical argument. Our pain pushes us to ask much more personal questions. What we really want to know is:

> Does God really care when bad things happen to me?
> Does He still love me?
> Does He even see what I am going through?
> Has God somehow forgotten me?
> Does He have any idea how much I hurt?

The answer to all those questions is yes. The answer is undeniably, unequivocally, unceasingly, *yes*.

Read the next five sentences carefully.

> God does care when bad things happen to you.
> He still loves you.
> He sees and feels your pain.
> He has not forgotten you.
> He knows more about suffering than you can imagine.

Remember, Jesus Knows Suffering

Read the description of the sufferings of our Savior slowly. Note the variety and intensity of the pain He endured.

> *He was despised and rejected by men, a man of*
> *sorrows, and familiar with suffering. Like one from*
> *whom men hide their faces he was despised, and we*
> *esteemed him not. Surely he took up our infirmities*
> *and carried our sorrows, yet we considered him*
> *stricken by God, smitten by him, and afflicted. But he*
> *was pierced for our transgressions, he was crushed for*
> *our iniquities; the punishment that brought us peace*
> *was upon him, and by his wounds we are healed. . . .*
> *He was oppressed and afflicted, yet he did not open his*
> *mouth; he was led like a lamb to the slaughter. . . .*
> *By oppression and judgment he was taken away. And*
> *who can speak of his descendants? For he was cut off*
> *from the land of the living; for the transgression of my*
> *people he was stricken. . . . Yet it was the LORD's will*
> *to crush him and cause him to suffer. . . . After the*
> *suffering of his soul, he will see the light of life and be*
> *satisfied; by his knowledge my righteous servant will*
> *justify many, and he will bear their iniquities.*
> ISAIAH 53:3–11

What are you experiencing that Jesus hasn't? Look again at those words: *infirmities, sorrows, stricken, smitten, afflicted, pierced, crushed, punishment, wounds, oppressed, afflicted, slaughter, oppression, cut off, stricken, crush, suffer,* and *suffering of his soul.* Jesus knows suffering.

The only One who did not deserve to suffer indeed suffered the uttermost to save us. In speaking of the sufferings of Jesus, the Bible says:

> *For we do not have a high priest who is unable to*
> *sympathize with our weaknesses, but we have one who*
> *has been tempted in every way, just as we are—yet*
> *was without sin. Let us then approach the throne of*
> *grace with confidence, so that we may receive mercy*
> *and find grace to help us in our time of need.*
> HEBREWS 4:15–16

Jesus understands the sufferings we experience. This makes Him an infinitely approachable deity and is yet another reminder that our God desires an intimate relationship with us.

My Eyes Have Seen You

Possibly nothing is as difficult for a parent as burying his or her child. Imagine—Job buried *ten* children at the same time. His heart was cruelly crushed by his immense grief. Yet, instead of lying in the dust and crying for himself, Job cried out to God. As you read his story, you encounter a man who sincerely bared his soul to God. It wasn't always pretty. His emotions were raw, his words angry. He yelled *at* God and he yelled *to* God. He questioned God.

But make no mistake: Job did not allow his pain to push him *from* God. Instead, he let it press him *to* God. Job came to God, and although He didn't do so immediately, God came to him (Job 38:1). God came in power, provision, affirmation, consolation, and ultimately blessing.

In Job's journey through the tunnel of adversity, he ended up confronting the fact that God's goal in allowing him to suffer was not the revelation of a rationale for Job's agony, but rather the revelation of God Himself. After avoiding Job for thirty-six chapters, as Job defended himself and requested an audience, when God finally did show up to speak with Job, He didn't give Job a list of reasons for the suffering. Instead, He gave Job a tour of His person and His power.

Seeing God through the lens of suffering gave Job a different, and ultimately closer, perspective of God. As I studied the book of Job, I was confronted and comforted with the fact that God's goal in suffering is not the revelation of reasons or explanations, but rather the revelation of Himself. Job wrote,

> *"My ears had heard of you but now my eyes have seen you."*
> JOB 42:5

Job went from having a hearsay relationship with God ("my ears had heard of you") to a face-to-face encounter ("but now my eyes have seen you"). Through suffering he went from a secondhand faith to a firsthand relationship.

So often when things are going well, we are too busy or too distracted to really see God. But when suffering narrows our options, the blinders of pain can force us to truly look at God. It is not until suffering throws us on our backs that we finally look up and see God.

Many of us would testify that we met God when we were pressed to Him through pain. Although raised in a God-fearing home, taken to church from birth, and sent to a Christian school, my mom did not meet God personally until she nearly died of pneumonia as a teenager. Suffering brought her closer to God.

God Comes to the Brokenhearted

God does not always come to every brokenhearted seeker in the same way, but He always comes. To Elijah, God came as a still small voice. To Jonah, God came through a vine and a voice. To Shadrach, Meshach, and Abednego, God came and stood with them in the furnace of fire. To the disciples, Jesus came walking on the waves in the middle of a storm. God can't keep from coming to brokenhearted seekers.

David recognized this when he was unjustly forced to live the life of a fugitive. He found himself the target of the biggest manhunt in Israel's history, as jealous King Saul led an entire army out to chase him down. He lost his home, job, career, friends, wife, and future. Constantly on the move, unsure of whom to trust, hiding in caves, running for his life, narrowly escaping death, David had to have wrestled with doubts of God's love. Nevertheless, he came to God, and God came to him at his lowest point. As a result, David proclaimed a precious promise.

> *The LORD is close to the brokenhearted and saves those*
> *who are crushed in spirit.*
> PSALM 34:18

This verse seems rather sweet and pleasant when you are not suffering. But when you are staring in disbelief at the smashed pieces of your broken heart or when you are enduring the helpless feeling of being crushed by sorrow, these words can be transformed into something of great comfort and tangible power. To you, this promise can be a lifeline, an anchor, and a foundation. As you are suffering, remember these four truths:

1. God does not abandon us when we suffer, although it often feels as if He does. No. He has been with us, will be with us, and is always with us. But He is closest to us when we hurt.
2. The presence of hardship does not mark the absence of God. A broken heart is irresistible to Him. God comes to the brokenhearted because He cannot help Himself. A crushed spirit is a magnet drawing Him close.
3. God does not promise to protect us from all problems, but He does promise to be with us through our problems.
4. It is really up to you. Adversity will either come between you and God or it will push you closer to God—it's your choice.

Companionship in the Ruins

Christian celebrity Sheila Walsh admitted herself as a patient to the psychiatric unit of a hospital in Washington, D.C. She was extremely afraid she would end up like her father, who died in his thirties in a bleak psychiatric hospital in Scotland. With the sensitivity that is only learned in the school of severe suffering, she writes:

> *I did not understand that God's most precious gifts*
> *come in boxes that make your hands bleed when you*
> *open them. Inside is what you have been looking*
> *for all of your life. Only God can do that. Only His*
> *love is as fierce and relentless as our deepest pain*
> *and unspoken fears. . . . I longed for rescue; He gave*
> *me relationship. I wanted deliverance; He gave me*
> *companionship in the ruins.*[1]

"Companionship in the ruins"—what a beautiful thought. Sounds reminiscent of the apostle Paul when he wrote, "That I may know Him, and the power of His resurrection, and *the fellowship of His sufferings*" (Philippians 3:10 NKJV, emphasis added). It also reminds me of the words of author Oswald Chambers when he prayed, "Pierce a hole in the darkness so that I can behold the face of God."

He Came So Near

In the mid-1800s, over one hundred thousand pioneers loaded all their possessions into covered wagons and ventured west. Walking fifteen miles a day, they attempted to travel the two thousand miles from Missouri to the Pacific Coast via the Oregon Trail. The journey west was extremely hard, and many turned back or did not survive.

Hardships were plentiful, from lack of good water to food shortages to real dangers. Crossing rivers was a constant headache to the pioneers. Many people drowned in the Kansas, North Platte, and Columbia rivers. Some died when they fell under the massive wheels of a wagon. Indians, outlaws, and cholera were also constant threats.

After a life-threatening trial on the trail, one pioneer wrote in her diary:

> *I had known what it was to believe in God, but now*
> *He came so near that I no longer simply believed in*

*Him but knew His presence there. . . . That calm
strength, that certainty of One near and all-sufficient,
hushed and cheered.*[2]

"He came so near." Her words are echoed by many of us who
have walked the path of pain.

Why?

So why does God allow bad things to happen to good people?
One reason is that we often experience the nearness of God more
in trial than in triumph. God is near to the brokenhearted.

Notes

1. Sheila Walsh, "A Winter's Tale," in *The Desert Experience: Personal
   Reflections on Finding God's Presence and Promise in Hard Times*
   (Nashville: Nelson, 2001), 172, 176.
2. From the diary of the mother of Josiah Royce, quoted in
   Donald Morgan, *How to Get It Together When Your World
   Is Coming Apart* (Grand Rapids: Revell, 1988), 18.

6

To Prepare Us to Receive Far Greater Blessings
JOB 42

In his book *The Dream Giver*, Bruce Wilkinson tells of the time he and his wife, Darlene Marie, launched a magazine by faith, obeying God at great personal cost. For five months he asked God to provide, and for five months God seemingly did nothing. Finding themselves in debt more than five years' salary, they called a meeting to shut down the magazine. For Wilkinson it was a crucifixion, the death of a dream. Later he describes what he called his "WasteLand" experience with these painful words:

> *It felt like God had watched from the sidelines while we went down in flames. It was one of the most disillusioning seasons of my life. . . . Before long, I felt adrift in anger and confusion.*[1]

Yet painful loss can lead to plentiful gain. Bruce observed:

> *It wasn't until years later that I could look back on that season and see that God had been faithfully at work. What we couldn't know then was that He had plans for a different kind of magazine,* The Daily Walk, *and He was preparing us to accomplish it. Today* Walk Thru the Bible *publishes ten magazines every month. . . . One hundred million devotional magazines later, it's clear God didn't let us down. God just had a bigger dream than we could have achieved or even imagined at the time.*[2]

Bruce became the publisher and executive editor of ten monthly magazines with distribution numbering over 120 million. Later he wrote a little book called *The Prayer of Jabez*. That book is the only book in history to win Evangelical Christian Publishers Association's "Book of the Year" two years in a row. *Publisher's Weekly* reported *The Prayer of Jabez* as the "fastest-selling book of all time" in 2001.[3]

Why does God allow bad things to happen to good people? Sometimes it is to position and prepare them for greater blessings.

Twice as Much after Prior Pain

I have read the book of Job dozens of times. My favorite chapter is the last. As you recall, the first two chapters tell us that Job, one of the richest men in the East, underwent one of the worst seasons of loss any individual has ever endured. He lost seven thousand head of sheep, three thousand camels, five hundred teams of oxen, five hundred donkeys, and a huge staff of servants. He also lost his ten children. So as a businessman and as a father, Job lost it all.

Thankfully for Job, the story did not end there. In the middle of the last chapter, God stretches a rainbow over the storm, and the sun bursts through the clouds. Notice carefully the second half of this verse.

> *After Job had prayed for his friends, the LORD made him prosperous again and gave him twice as much as he had before.*
> JOB 42:10

Do you see what happened? The Lord did not merely return everything back to Job. No. The Lord gave Job *twice as much as he had before!* Why does God allow bad things to happen? Sometimes He seems to be preparing us for a greater blessing.

What is interesting is that when the Bible says that Job received *twice* as much, it means literally *twice* as much. Look at the rest of the chapter.

> *The LORD blessed the latter part of Job's life more
> than the first. He had fourteen thousand sheep, six
> thousand camels, a thousand yoke of oxen and
> a thousand donkeys.*
>
> JOB 42:12

Prior to suffering, Job had seven thousand head of sheep; he ended up with fourteen thousand. He had three thousand camels; he ended up with six thousand. He had five hundred teams of oxen; after suffering, he had one thousand. He had five hundred donkeys; he finished with one thousand. But there was more.

> *And he also had seven sons and three daughters. . . .
> Nowhere in all the land were there found women as
> beautiful as Job's daughters.*
>
> JOB 42:13, 15

You may be thinking, *But I thought Job had ten children prior to the tragedy. Why did the Lord not give him twice as many, which would be twenty kids?* The answer is that the loss of Job's first ten children was only temporary. He was to be reunited with the first ten in heaven.

Oh, by the way, Job also received twice the life span of an ordinary man added on to his life. Instead of living the normal seventy years, the Bible says, "After this, Job lived a hundred and forty years; he saw his children and their children to the fourth generation" (Job 42:16).

Because Job's response to suffering was relentless worship, the results of his suffering were such amazing gains as a bigger perspective of God, greater intimacy with God, and deeper humility before God. Also, God was able to bless Job with twice the number of earthly blessings he had before. Sometimes God may be allowing bad things into your life to prepare you to handle greater blessings.

Are You Really Ready for Success?

Most of us have dreamed of having amazing wealth and incredible influence, but we need to be reminded that vast amounts of money and power ruin the unprepared. You may think winning the lottery would solve your problems, but it might just expose, deepen, and escalate them.

Have you noticed? Most of us are much better able to handle success *after* we have tasted failure. The hard lessons learned through the tough times ready us to deal with better days by building into our lives needed virtues such as grace, dependence, and perspective. Bad times produce good things in us that mold us into the type of people God can trust to handle more good things.

Preparation for Greater Ministry Impact

Charles Spurgeon is considered "the prince of preachers." He was the first to regularly speak to crowds of multiple thousands Sunday after Sunday at his Metropolitan Tabernacle in London in the nineteenth century. He authored two hundred books. Yet during his adult life he battled painful gout and deep seasons of depression. He felt his hardship kept him humble and dependent on the Lord. With great insight he wrote:

> *Uninterrupted success and unfading joy in it would be more than our weak heads could bear. . . . My witness is, that those who are honored by their Lord in public have usually to endure a secret chastening, or to carry a peculiar cross, lest by any means they exalt themselves, and fall into the snare of the devil.*[4]

His experience was that misery was often the precursor to prosperity, buffeting the bridge to blessing. Given his familiarity with the formula, Spurgeon wrote:

> *Depression comes over me whenever the Lord is*
> *preparing a larger blessing for my ministry. It has now*
> *become to me a prophet in rough clothing. . . . Before*
> *any great achievement, some measure of the same*
> *depression is very usual.[5]*

Twice as Much without Prior Pain

A funny thing happens when a human suddenly experiences great wealth without the preparation that comes through prior pain. It does not make them any happier and often makes things worse. "Though buying power has more than doubled since the 1950s, the average American's reported happiness has remained almost unchanged," concluded Hope College professor David G. Meyers after analyzing data from National Opinion Research Center surveys and income data from *Historical Statistics of the United States* and *Economic Indicators*. He further states:

> *The average American, though certainly richer, is not*
> *a bit happier. In 1957, some 35 percent said they were*
> *"very happy," as did slightly fewer—30 percent—in*
> *2002. Indeed, if we can judge from statistics—a*
> *doubled divorce rate, more-than-doubled teen*
> *suicide, and mushrooming depression—contemporary*
> *Americans seem to be more often miserable.[6]*

Losing by Winning

Job lost much, but he ultimately won more. Often, however, people who win much will lose even more. Few of us are really ready to receive greater blessing. Without the process of pain, we are unprepared for prosperity.

For example, a surprisingly high number of lottery winners end up worse off financially than they were before they won. Nearly one-third of multimillion-dollar lottery winners are bankrupt within a few years.[7]

Money alone can't buy happiness, and winning the lottery does not make people happier. One famous study measured the happiness of lottery winners against people who were recently paralyzed. The study found no measurable difference in happiness between the two groups.[8]

Many think that winning the lottery could solve their problems. Guess again. The evidence clearly indicates that gaining prosperity without developing the necessary values and character that come through hardship and suffering can be devastating.

Ask "Bud" Post, who won $16.2 million in a 1988 lottery. He now lives on his Social Security. "I wish it never happened. It was totally a nightmare," says Post. His former girlfriend successfully sued him for a share of his winnings. A brother was arrested for hiring a hit man to kill him, hoping to inherit a share of Post's winnings. His other siblings pestered him until he agreed to invest in ventures that made no money and further strained his relationship with them. Eventually, Post spent time in jail. Within a year, he was $1 million in debt. Today he lives on food stamps.[9]

Ask Evelyn Adams. She won the New Jersey lottery not just once, but twice (1985, 1986). Her total winnings numbered $5.4 million. Today, all her money is gone and she lives in a trailer. "Winning the lottery isn't always what it's cracked up to be," she said. "I won the American dream but I lost it, too. It was a very hard fall. It's called rock bottom."[10]

Receiving huge amounts of money often compounds problems for some people. Ask Jack Whittaker. He won the largest undivided lottery jackpot in U.S. history, $113 million. When he won, newspapers carried pictures of Jack, the boisterous, happy-go-lucky, respected contractor. Two years later they carried his mug shot as a haggard, somber man who had been arrested twice on drunken driving charges within a year and had been ordered into rehab. He also went to court for charges that he attacked a bar manager, and he was accused in two lawsuits of making trouble at a nightclub and a racetrack.[11]

God knows that the vast majority of us could never handle

the sudden receipt of a large amount of money. We need to experience pain prior to being prepared for prosperity. He also knows that few can handle great ministry blessings without growing self-sufficient and proud. He develops our character and our humble dependency on Him through hardship. Buffeting prepares us for blessing.

Why?

Why would a good God allow His children to experience bad things? It might be to prepare us to receive greater blessings. Maybe the suffering you are enduring is part of God's plan to prepare you for greater blessings.

Notes

1. Bruce Wilkinson, *The Dream Giver* (Sisters, OR: Multnomah, 2003), 114.
2. Ibid., 115.
3. http://www.brucewilkinson.com/meetbruce.html (accessed February 18, 2007).
4 As quoted in Helmut Thielicke, John Doberstein, trans., *Encounter with Spurgeon* (Grand Rapids: Baker, 1975), 214.
5. Richard E. Day, *The Shadow of the Broad Brim* (Philadelphia: Judson, 1934), 175.
6. David G. Meyers, "Happiness," http://www.davidmyers.org/Brix?pageID=48 (accessed October 21, 2006).
7. Sherri Granato, "Winning the Lottery: Curse or Blessing?" http://www.associatedcontent.com/article/70165/winning_the_lottery_curse_or_a_blessing.html (accessed October 21, 2006).
8. Philip Brickman, Dan D. Coates, and Ronnie J. Janoff-Bulman, "Lottery Winners and Accident Victims: Is Happiness Relative?", http://www.ncbi.nlm.nih.gov/entrez/query.gcgi?cmd=Retrieve&db=PubMed&list_uids=690806&dopt=Abstract (accessed October 21, 2006).
9. Ellen Goodstein, "8 Lottery Winners Who Lost Their Millions," Bankrate.com, http://articles.moneycentral.msn.com/SavingandDebt/SaveMoney/8lotteryWinnersWhoLostTheirMillions.aspx (accessed October 21, 2006).
10. Ibid.
11. Kelley Schoonover, "For Lottery Winner 113m Hasn't Brought Happiness," Associated Press, December 14, 2004, http://www.boston.com/news/nation/articles/2004/12/14/lottery_winner_113m_hasnt_bought_happiness/.

To Position Us for Higher Promotion
GENESIS 50:20

How on earth could a Hebrew shepherd, the eleventh-ranked brother in his own family, possibly become prime minister of a mighty world power? Humanly speaking it would be absolutely, undeniably, irrevocably impossible. But there is a God who can use very bad things to accomplish very good things, even impossibly good things—and that is exactly what happened to a boy named Joe. This is his story.

Bad Things

A somewhat precocious teenager, seventeen-year-old Joseph awoke one morning thrilled yet fearful. That night he had dreamed a very clear dream of becoming a leader. He was convinced that God had pulled back the veil and had given him a glimpse of his destiny. God was calling him to a life of leadership.

Excitedly, Joseph shared with his already jealous older brothers his dream of eventually being leader of the family. This was not wise. Their envy turned to bitter hatred, and they waited for a chance to punish him. Bad things were about to happen to a good person.

Opportunity soon presented itself. Joseph was doing what his father had asked when he went to get a report on how his brothers were getting along grazing the flocks fifty miles away from the family compound. Unsuspectingly, Joseph walked into a trap. His jealous brothers grabbed him, threw him into an empty well, and were planning to leave him for dead. Eventually,

Joseph's eldest brother convinced the others to sell him to a caravan of slave traders.

Just like that, his wonderful dream turned to a horrible nightmare. Betrayed and abused by his own brothers, he was left for dead, then sold into slavery. Why did a good God allow such a bad thing to happen to a good boy?

Son Becomes a Slave

What an awful event to occur, especially at the hands of his own brothers! One day Joseph had been the favored son of a wealthy shepherd; the next he was a slave. All his possessions, rights, and privileges were taken. He was nothing more than a commodity, a piece of property, in the hands of evil men. Where was God?

Eventually, the caravan stopped in Egypt, a bizarre land on the Nile River. Potiphar, the captain of Pharaoh's guard, bought Joseph and put him to work serving his large household.

Joseph's life began to look up. He refused to become bitter toward God. He worked hard. Soon he began to display leadership skills. Little by little he gained Potiphar's trust, and his role expanded until he was put in charge of managing the household. Far from home in a strange place, in the lowly position of slave, Joseph was learning how to lead. Good things were starting to happen.

Then everything came crashing down.

More Bad Things

Joseph was an attractive young man, and he caught the eye of Potiphar's wife. The lustful woman tried to seduce Joseph. In his loyalty to God and his master, he repeatedly rebuffed her advances. He did the right thing. You might expect God to bless him with good things because of his faithful obedience in the face of stiff testing, yet it was not to be. More very bad things happened to a very good person.

Scorned and vengeful, the awful woman accused Joseph of attempting to rape her. It was the word of the Egyptian wife of a high-ranking official against that of a foreign slave. Joseph stood no chance. The next thing he knew, Joseph found himself in prison. Sorrow was heaped on sorrow. If it had not been bad enough to be a slave, now he was a convict. Why was God allowing such bad things to happen to such a good man?

Bad Becomes Worse

Initially, Joseph's predicament contained a thread of promise. His work ethic and leadership were put to good use, and he was given opportunity to develop as a servant leader. Joseph was privileged to associate with a few of Pharaoh's formerly high-ranking political prisoners. They discussed life in the palace and the challenges of leading the nation. Good things were starting to happen.

Joseph's position in prison afforded him the usual opportunity of predicting that the king's ex-cupbearer would be restored to his former position. In making the prediction, Joseph hoped that the cupbearer would champion Joseph's unfair plight and plead his case on the outside. Maybe he would be freed from the prison.

But days turned to weeks. Weeks stretched into years. The cupbearer forgot him. Joseph's dream of freedom died.

How bad could it get? He was unfairly rejected by his family, unsuspectingly sold into slavery, and unjustly thrown into prison. Now he was forgotten, left to rot behind bars. Ever since he had been given that cursed dream, Joseph had known one terrible event after another.

Where was God? Why did God allow such extremely awful things to happen to Joseph? What had Joseph done to deserve such severe suffering and sorrow? Didn't God care? What was God doing?

As it turned out, God had it under control every step of the way.

Dream becomes Destiny

One fateful night, Pharaoh sat up in bed soaked in sweat, unable to escape the dreams that had haunted his sleep. He called in his advisers, but they were dumbfounded by his odd dreams. Lacking an interpreter for Pharaoh's dream, suddenly the cupbearer remembered what Joseph had done in interpreting his dream. So the cupbearer told Pharaoh about Joseph.

Immediately, Pharaoh called Joseph in and recounted his bizarre dream. Patiently Joseph listened, quietly asking God for direction. With God-given skill, Joseph interpreted Pharaoh's dream as a prediction from God of imminent years of extreme famine.

Astutely, Joseph also laid out a simple plan for avoiding the deadly destruction of the famine by stockpiling provisions. Deeply impressed by Joseph's ability not only to interpret the dreams, but also to detail a solution, Pharaoh acted.

With his authority as emperor of Egypt, Pharaoh stunned the world by proclaiming Joseph the prime minister of the entire nation. Talk about an unlikely and unbelievable promotion! A Hebrew slave and imprisoned alleged rapist was made the second most powerful ruler of the most powerful nation on the planet in one moment!

In his new role, Joseph carefully stockpiled provisions. Of all the nations of the Middle East, only Egypt was prepared when the horrible famine hit. Joseph fed his people, made a rich profit selling grain to the nations, and saved the lives of many people, including his family. He saw thirteen years of truly terrible experiences swept away by the dizzying good that God accomplished in, for, and through him—good that never would have occurred without the help of the bad.

Good Things Out of the Bad

I love this story. Like a wise master patiently placing together pieces of a puzzle to form a stunningly beautiful picture, God used every bit of bad that Joseph experienced to position him for the highest possible promotion and greatest possible good. Wow! Only God could use the awful, ugly pain of kidnapping, slavery, and prison to so providentially prepare and position a boy to fulfill his wildest dreams *and* save many people's lives *and* save the Hebrew race from starving.

Why does God allow bad things to happen to good people? Sometimes it is to position them for greater promotion. God is big enough to accomplish incredibly good results from very bad events. Think back through Joseph's life.

- By serving as a slave managing Potiphar's house and as a prisoner running a prison, Joseph learned more about leadership than he would have back home.
- It was only by being in prison that Joseph was able to meet some former cabinet officials and was thus strategically placed to be available to explain Pharaoh's dream.
- As a result of being sold into slavery to a caravan who took him to Egypt, Joseph was divinely positioned to ultimately serve as prime minister of Egypt, the most influential nation on earth at that time.

None of the positive things in Joseph's life would have or could have happened without the negative. Why had God allowed those bad things to happen to a good man?

> *Skillfully, like a master weaver, using widely diverse pieces, ugly events, evil people, unjust treatment, and long periods of obscurity, God had woven all these things into a very beautiful tapestry. Like an elite chef, He cooked up a delicious stew out of the old vegetables, overlooked*

spices, and forgotten leftovers languishing in the pantry of Joseph's life. God turned very bad things into great good.[1]

Redirection

During my junior year in high school I had a very successful wrestling season. Several colleges began pursuing me with the potential of scholarship offers. I had totally committed my life to God and hoped to use my athletic ability to bring glory to His name.

Yet, in my senior year I tore up my knee midseason. My big dreams were rudely shattered. Not only was my injury painful and frustrating, but it brought an abrupt end to the potential scholarships. I was bummed out by my misfortune but tried to maintain faith that God would work the situation for good.

Why did God allow a bad thing to happen to me when I was trying so hard to do life right? Now I can see that at least one reason was to redirect my path. I ended up wrestling at a Christian college, something I was not considering prior to my injury. While there I met Cathy, the girl who would become my wife, and I was called and trained for a life of ministry, as well.

God brought good out of bad. He used my injury to redirect me to a different college and a different career than I would have discovered otherwise. I now see that God used my injury, and the resulting disappointment, to place me where I needed to be for what He had ahead.

Why does God allow bad things to happen to good people? Sometimes it is to better position them for a promotion. Many businesspeople have told me of being unfairly passed over for promotions, or even being unjustly fired, only to later realize that God had used that trial to strategically place them in a much better job.

Why?

Why would God allow negative events to overtake His own people? He might do so to position them for a greater promotion.

Note

1.   Dave Earley, *The 21 Most Encouraging Promises in the Bible* (Uhrichsville, OH: Barbour, 2005), 50.

8

To Prepare Us for the Miraculous
2 CHRONICLES 20

"How do you define a miracle?" my friend asked in a very soft voice.

"I have heard it defined as the unusual intervention of God by which the ordinary laws, course, and operation of nature are overruled, suspended, or modified. Why?"

In a reverent voice and with teary eyes, he gulped and answered, "Because I believe I have experienced one."

Two months prior to that conversation, my good friend Dr. Daniel Mitchell had been diagnosed with pancreatic cancer. Since pancreatic cancer is almost always lethal, the news of the cancer had been quite a shock to Dan, his family, and everyone who knew him. The thought of losing the beloved theology professor and academic dean for the seminary was heartbreaking, and we prayed for a miracle. Many wept, prayed, and feebly tried to encourage his wife, Nancy. Dan, however, was amazingly calm. After a few weeks of initial struggle, Dan was remarkably confident in the fact that God would do what was best.

That week he had endured a daunting battery of strenuous tests the doctors had ordered and awaited the results. Amazed at what the physicians had seen, his doctor gave him the verdict. What was thought to be a cancerous tumor on his X-rays was now only a shadow on the scan.

Dan was given a completely clean bill of health by his doctors. His story proves that God is still in the miracle-working business![1]

No Messes, No Miracles

> *When God is going to do something wonderful, He begins with a difficulty. If He is going to do something very wonderful, He begins with a mess.[2]*

Would you like God to do an amazing, jaw-dropping, inexplicable, stand up and holler miracle in your life? Who wouldn't want to see sickness instantaneously healed? Who wouldn't want to see a healthy child placed in a barren womb? What about a dead man made alive? How about walking on top of a stormy sea? How about clean, bubbling torrents of water in the desert? Think before you answer.

One day, as I was studying the miracles in the Bible, I had a profound insight. To you it is probably obvious, but to me it was a new understanding and a big deal. My big brainstorm was this: *There are no miracles without messes.*

Walk through the scriptures. Every miracle followed closely on the heels of a giant mess. For example:

- Sarah endured ninety years of the frustrating humiliation of barrenness *before* her miracle baby, Isaac, was born.
- Moses was leading a million slaves to their slaughter at the hands of Pharaoh and his chariots *before* the Red Sea opened, allowing them to pass through on dry land.
- Thousands of people had to grow tired and hungry *before* Jesus multiplied fish and bread enough for all to feast.
- The widow and her son had to be starving *ahead of* the unlimited bin of flour and unending jar of oil. Yet the flour and oil both ran out when no longer needed.
- Daniel had to be thrown into the lion's den *before* he could be spared from even a scratch.

- Shadrach, Meshach, and Abednego were thrown into the furnace *prior to* being protected so completely by the Son of God that no one could even smell smoke on them.
- Bartimaeus had to experience a lifetime of blindness *prior to* experiencing the Great Physician's healing touch.
- Jesus never would have had to free the man in the tombs from a legion of demons if the man had not been demonized in the first place.
- The ten lepers had to experience leprosy *before* experiencing the miracle of their healing.
- Peter had to go prison *before* the angel could unlock his chains and set him free.
- *Prior* to the amazing earthquake that opened the heart of the Philippian jailer, Paul and Silas had to go to jail.
- Lazarus had to die *before* he could rise from the dead! So did Jesus.

The biblical record is quite clear. There are no miracles without previous messes. The need for a miracle is necessitated by the presence of an impossible situation, usually unbearable suffering.

One Man's Miracle

Maybe you have been there. You were doing everything right. You were living as good and godly as you knew how. Yet suddenly, a heavy, sinister cloud darkened the sky. It blocked all hope from view. The odds were much too steep, the situation seemed impossible. You found yourself helplessly adrift in a huge mess. The only way out was a miracle.

King Jehoshaphat and his nation, Judah, were there. He had worked diligently to turn his people back to God. He was a good and godly man. Yet suddenly, three big, bloodthirsty armies allied themselves against him and breathed down the skinny neck of his lone army. A sea of evil invaders had amassed to sweep into Jerusalem like a terrible tide. He had a massive, ugly mess.

What could he do? Surrender meant certain slavery. Fighting meant definite defeat and death. What he needed was an undeniable, jaw-dropping, almost unbelievable, flat-out miracle.

When we experience the imminent threat of great pain and total loss, we always face a choice: We can run to God and trust Him or turn from Him and run away.

Take Your Problems to the Lord

Jehoshaphat ran to God. He turned his problems into prayer. I don't know if he prayed because he was a giant in the faith or just a coward with nowhere else to turn. It doesn't matter. What does matter is that he turned his greatest problem into his greatest prayer and added fasting. Wisely, he invited all of Judah to join him. Recognizing the desperate enormity of their plight, people came from all over Judah to join the prayer (2 Chronicles 20:3–13).

Jehoshaphat came to God with raw honesty, abject hopelessness, and naked humility in his request. In essence he said to God, "We are powerless. We don't know what to do. But we are looking to You!"

God is tenderhearted and is attracted to bare-boned brokenness. Such requests may not always get us what we want, but they put us on the path to getting what God wants.

I am a journal keeper. When I reread my journals, I find that the one prayer I pray most often consists of but three short, simple sentences. "I can't. You can. Please do." It is a good thing to give your problems to the Problem Solver. He can handle them.

The Battle Belongs to the Lord

Sometimes when we ask for miracles, God's wise response is silence. God sees that for us, at that time, deliverance is not best. But happily this is not always the case, and it wasn't the case for

Jehoshaphat and Judah. In response to their desperate prayer, God gave them a speedy and amazingly encouraging reply.

> *"The battle is not yours but God's. . . . You will not*
> *have to fight this battle. Take up your positions;*
> *stand firm and see the deliverance the* Lord *will give*
> *you. . .and the* Lord *will be with you."*
> 2 Chronicles 20:15, 17

Praise Warfare

God had promised them a miracle, but they had to actively believe Him. So Jehoshaphat unveiled his Praise Warfare battle plan. It would be a symbol of their active faith in their living God.

> *Early in the morning they left for the Desert of Tekoa.*
> *As they set out, Jehoshaphat stood and said, "Listen to*
> *me, Judah and people of Jerusalem! Have faith in the*
> Lord *your God and you will be upheld; have faith in*
> *his prophets and you will be successful." After consulting*
> *the people, Jehoshaphat appointed men to sing to the*
> Lord *and to praise him for the splendor of his holiness*
> *as they went out at the head of the army, saying: "Give*
> *thanks to the* Lord, *for his love endures forever."*
> 2 Chronicles 20:20–21

The Real Battle

I wish I had been there that morning. I can only imagine being one of the musicians or singers, who usually watched battles from a safe distance in the rear. But now they were to line up in the front row of the army. Imagine the wild thoughts and reckless fear that must have brewed just below the surface of their minds. *This is insane. Unless God comes through, we are marching out like sheep to be slaughtered. We'll be singing, "Give thanks to the Lord," and they'll by cutting off our heads.*

Consider what thoughts must have been knocking at the doors of the minds of the Judean soldiers. *This is crazy. Those dumb singers are just going to be in the way. The only good thing is that maybe after killing all of them, the bad guys will be tired. But we still won't have a chance.*

We can guess what Jehoshaphat's cabinet members were thinking. *The old man has finally flipped out. March into battle singing praises? This plan stands no chance. I hope they will just make us slaves instead of examples.*

The biggest battle the Judeans faced was not fighting their foes, but fighting their fears. It was really a battle to believe. Often it is much tougher to fight invisible fear than visible enemies. Why did God allow them to get in this situation in the first place? One reason was that He wanted to test and strengthen their faith.

Fortunately, faith faced down fears. They lined up and marched out, singing praises to their Warrior God—and it worked!

God Wins!

> *As they began to sing and praise, the LORD set ambushes against the men of Ammon and Moab and Mount Seir who were invading Judah, and they were defeated. The men of Ammon and Moab rose up against the men from Mount Seir to destroy and annihilate them. After they finished slaughtering the men from Seir, they helped to destroy one another.*
>
> 2 CHRONICLES 20:22–23

I love this story. It was only *as* they began to sing and praise that God got busy ambushing the evil invaders. And ambush them He did. The enemy became so confused that they turned on one another. The next thing you know they had destroyed each other.

It probably took but a few hours at most for the men of Judea to gather together, line up, and march to the place overlooking the desert where the invaders had camped. Yet it took them three days to gather the plunder (2 Chronicles 20:25)!

But there is more. In one morning, God had not merely blessed and grown the Judeans' faith, He had not only given them a huge amount of free goodies, but He also so totally defeated Judea's nearest enemies that other potential enemies decided to stay away, as well (2 Chronicles 20:29–30). The nation enjoyed an extended period of peace.

But beyond all that, this sensational story of a miraculous victory has been recorded in our Bibles and has been the source of immense encouragement for an untold number of believers for thousands of years.

Don't miss the most glaring fact in this true story. The glorious miracle and these great by-products would never have, could never have, occurred without the enemy invaders breathing invincibly down their necks in the first place. Why did God allow a good king like Jehoshaphat to face such a bad thing as a bloody invasion and pending destruction? Why did an all-loving, all-powerful God allow such a massive mess in the first place? Because He knows there are no miracles without messes.

Why?

Everyone wants miracles, but we must never forget that miracles do not come without messes. People cannot be healed unless they are first sick or broken. Bills cannot be paid unless there are bills needing to be paid. There is no need for miracles until people find themselves in impossibly painful messes.

Why does God allow bad things to happen to good people? Sometimes it is in preparation for a miracle.

Notes

1. Daniel Mitchell's story is used by permission.
2. Dewey Cass, quoted in Tim Hansel, *Through the Wilderness of Loneliness* (Elgin, IL: Cook, 1991), 18.

To Increase the Testimony of God

DANIEL 6

Daniel was an amazingly good and godly person who was an excellent administrator. His boss, King Darius, was so impressed with Daniel that he intended to appoint Daniel as prime minister, his right-hand man. Daniel would be in charge of the entire massive kingdom of the Medes and Persians.

But the other administrators were jealous of Daniel, and they began to plot a way to get rid of him. However, he was so competent and his record was so clean that the only accusation they could think of to use against him was his faith in the living God. So they came up with a devious scheme. They would play to the king's ego and trap Daniel at the same time. Brilliant! Read what they did:

> So the administrators and the satraps went as a group
> to the king and said: "O King Darius, live forever!
> The royal administrators, prefects, satraps, advisers and
> governors have all agreed that the king should issue an
> edict and enforce the decree that anyone who prays to
> any god or man during the next thirty days, except to
> you, O king, shall be thrown into the lions' den. Now,
> O king, issue the decree and put it in writing so that
> it cannot be altered—in accordance with the laws of
> the Medes and Persians, which cannot be repealed."
> So King Darius put the decree in writing.
> DANIEL 6:6–9

They did not underestimate Daniel or his faithfulness to God. When he learned of the decree, Daniel did exactly as he had done before, continuing to pray three times a day to his God. Together, his enemies came to find him praying, and they gleefully took the news to the king. Their evil plan was falling into place very nicely.

> *So they went to the king and spoke to him about his royal decree: "Did you not publish a decree that during the next thirty days anyone who prays to any god or man except to you, O king, would be thrown into the lions' den?"*
>
> *The king answered, "The decree stands—in accordance with the laws of the Medes and Persians, which cannot be repealed."*
>
> DANIEL 6:12

Understandably, the king was upset that Daniel was caught in the wicked web. Yet the decrees of the king of the Medes and Persians could not be repealed by anyone, including the king himself. He had no choice. He had to send Daniel to his death.

> *So the king gave the order, and they brought Daniel and threw him into the lions' den. The king said to Daniel, "May your God, whom you serve continually, rescue you!"*
>
> *A stone was brought and placed over the mouth of the den, and the king sealed it with his own signet ring and with the rings of his nobles, so that Daniel's situation might not be changed.*
>
> DANIEL 6:16–17

The Rest of the Story

Stop. Think about what happened. Daniel was a good man who was sentenced to death for doing a good thing, faithfully standing for God and praying to Him no matter what. Why did a good and almighty God permit this horrible event to happen to such a truly good person? Let's find out.

> At the first light of dawn, the king got up and hurried to the lions' den. When he came near the den, he called to Daniel in an anguished voice, "Daniel, servant of the living God, has your God, whom you serve continually, been able to rescue you from the lions?"
>
> Daniel answered, "O king, live forever! My God sent his angel, and he shut the mouths of the lions. They have not hurt me, because I was found innocent in his sight. Nor have I ever done any wrong before you, O king."
>
> The king was overjoyed and gave orders to lift Daniel out of the den. And when Daniel was lifted from the den, no wound was found on him, because he had trusted in his God.
>
> DANIEL 6:19–23

Wow! God allowed such a big mess so He could do such a great miracle. No one lived through a night in the lions' den, but Daniel did. No one could hope to survive even a minute or two in the lions' den without being hopelessly maimed and mangled, if not severely cut and injured, but Daniel did. His God had delivered him.

But that is not the end of the story. Read on.

> At the king's command, the men who had falsely accused Daniel were brought in and thrown into the lions' den, along with their wives and children. And before they reached the floor of the den, the lions overpowered them and crushed all their bones.
>
> DANIEL 6:24

I love it when the bad guys get it in the end. But there is more. It gets better. Darius issued a new decree that trumped the old one.

> *Then King Darius wrote to all the peoples, nations and men of every language throughout the land:*
> *"May you prosper greatly! I issue a decree that in every part of my kingdom people must fear and reverence the God of Daniel. For he is the living God and he endures forever; his kingdom will not be destroyed, his dominion will never end. He rescues and he saves; he performs signs and wonders in the heavens and on the earth. He has rescued Daniel from the power of the lions."*
> *So Daniel prospered during the reign of Darius and the reign of Cyrus the Persian.*
> DANIEL 6:25–28

The Big Picture

A big, ugly, evil thing happened to Daniel. He was unjustly plotted against and, as a result, was thrown into the lions' den for being faithful to his God. Yet God turned this one great evil into many greater goods.

- Daniel was spared.
- Daniel's enemies were destroyed.
- Daniel was securely set up for the rest of his life.
- The king received a mighty witness of the power of God and His love for His children.
- Religious freedom for all of the Jews was greatly expanded.
- And best of all, the entire nation was told that they needed to fear and reverence the God of Daniel!

Why did God allow a good and godly man, Daniel, to experience such a horrible incident? The reasons were manifold and the blessings abundant. Yeah, God!

The Bigger Picture

God's ultimate plan behind all of His activities on this planet is to present humanity with a clear testimony of who He truly is and what He does. While Daniel's situation impacted his life and future, it went well beyond that. An entire generation of pagans and Jews living in the most powerful kingdom on earth received a strong witness of the immense glory of the living God. Who knows how many of those people turned to God or were better able to live for Him because Daniel went to the lions' den? Beyond that, how many of us, through the past thousands of years, have had our faith strengthened by reading the true story of Daniel and the lions' den?

The Same Story Acted Out with Different Actors

What happened to Daniel is not unique. Several years prior, when the Babylonian king Nebuchadnezzar was on the throne, three of Daniel's Hebrew friends—you know their names: Shadrach, Meshach, and Abednego—faced a similar situation. They could either bow down to an idol made in the likeness of the king or be executed. Like Daniel, they refused to bow to anyone other than the living God. As a result, they were thrown into a red-hot furnace, heated hotter than ever before.

Again, a bad thing happened to good people because they were faithful to God. Again, God miraculously intervened.

> *Then King Nebuchadnezzar leaped to his feet in*
> *amazement and asked his advisers, "Weren't there*
> *three men that we tied up and threw into the fire?"*
> *They replied, "Certainly, O king."*
> *He said, "Look! I see four men walking around in*
> *the fire, unbound and unharmed, and the fourth looks*
> *like a son of the gods."*
> *Nebuchadnezzar then approached the opening of*
> *the blazing furnace and shouted, "Shadrach, Meshach*

and Abednego, servants of the Most High God, come out! Come here!"

So Shadrach, Meshach and Abednego came out of the fire, and the satraps, prefects, governors and royal advisers crowded around them. They saw that the fire had not harmed their bodies, nor was a hair of their heads singed; their robes were not scorched, and there was no smell of fire on them.

DANIEL 3:24–27

Again, God used His turning of evil into good to provide a clear and powerful testimony of His glory. Again, laws were changed to advance His worship. And again, His people ended up with greater prosperity and promotion than they would have otherwise experienced! Yeah, God!

Then Nebuchadnezzar said, "Praise be to the God of Shadrach, Meshach and Abednego, who has sent his angel and rescued his servants! They trusted in him and defied the king's command and were willing to give up their lives rather than serve or worship any god except their own God. Therefore I decree that the people of any nation or language who say anything against the God of Shadrach, Meshach and Abednego be cut into pieces and their houses be turned into piles of rubble, for no other god can save in this way."

Then the king promoted Shadrach, Meshach and Abednego in the province of Babylon.

DANIEL 3:28–30

Bad to Good in the Twenty-first Century

Matt, my good friend and a young man I have mentored, was called to start a new church across the city from our church. He saw firsthand how God could turn a potentially devastating situation into a blessing for the entire community.

His brand-new church, New Life Church, began meeting in a privately owned banquet facility. One month later, Matt received a "cease and desist" letter from city zoning officials requiring the church to immediately cease meeting at their current location. The reason given was that they were in violation of zoning code, and if they did not comply, they would be criminally charged for every meeting.

The church believed it had a constitutional right to assemble together, so they did not cease worshipping on Sundays. Matt sought counsel from the Bible and claimed the truth found in Acts 5:38–39.

> *"Therefore, in the present case I advise you: Leave these men alone! Let them go! For if their purpose or activity is of human origin, it will fail. But if it is from God, you will not be able to stop these men; you will only find yourselves fighting against God."*

In the weeks following, things got worse. The owner of the banquet hall faced criminal charges for allowing the church to meet in his facilities. The city's law director even publicly compared the church to an organization renting the place to sell illegal drugs. The unrelenting oppression forced the church and banquet hall to file a joint federal lawsuit against the city in order to retain the right for the church to assemble together.

That's when God stepped in to turn the tables and bless many. When the church had begun, zoning legislation did not allow for *any* new church buildings. Consequently, no new church buildings had been built in the city for more than twenty-five years. However, when the lawsuit wrapped up (out of court), the city had modified its zoning code. Today, church gatherings and church buildings are allowed in nearly every part of the city![1]

Why?

So why would God allow very good people to go through very trying times and stifling situations? Sometimes He uses it to accomplish much greater good and spread His testimony farther than it would have spread otherwise.

Note

1. Story used by permission of Matt Chittum, pastor of New Life Church, Hilliard, Ohio (http://www.newlife.us/).

To Bring Us to Himself
ACTS 16

He dreamed of a good life, a good job, and a good family. He was just a few months from retirement. Things had fallen into place and were going his way—until the night all his dreams were shaken and shattered.

Earlier in the day, he had taken into custody two political prisoners. Religious zealots, they had incited a riot. He did not know all the details, but somehow these terrible two claimed to have cast a demon out of a slave girl in the name of Jesus. They had been dragged before the authorities and severely whipped and beaten. That's when they were turned over to him.

He locked them into the inner cell and fastened their feet in stocks. He would sleep soundly tonight. No one could get out of there. Or so he thought.

Unlike most prisoners, moaning and crying, these crazy men started praying and singing praises to Jesus. They weren't great singers, but their singing was interesting and did sound pretty nice. . .and harmless—he thought. So he went to sleep.

Suddenly, the ground started pitching and the walls began shaking. An earthquake was taking place right under the cell of those two religious men. Miraculously, all the prison doors flew open and all the chains came loose. No one was hurt.

How had this happened? What had he done wrong? All his hopes and dreams were gone, completely gone.

Trembling, the jailer knew what he had to do. Allowing prisoners to escape was unacceptable. When he accepted the job, he knew the policy. For a jailer to lose a prisoner was to lose his life. So resolutely he grabbed his sword and drew it out before his stomach. One quick plunge and it would be over.

Good-bye wife, good-bye kids, good-bye world.

"Stop!" a voice broke his concentration.

"Don't harm yourself. We are all here." It was those two men.

Stunned, amazed, relieved, overjoyed, afraid—the man called for a light. Running into their cell, he found the two men concerned, calm, unhurt, and smiling. Happily, he led these miracle producers out into the room where his family was eagerly gathered. They were confused and relieved. They had assumed that the jailer would have killed himself by now. But there he was, standing before them with the two smiling men.

"Sirs," he asked the men through trembling lips, "what must I do to be saved?"

"Believe on the Lord Jesus, and you will be saved," one answered. Then gesturing to the man's family, he added, "You and your family."

They did believe on the Lord Jesus and proved it by being baptized (for the full account, read Acts 16:16–40). One reason these good men, Paul and Silas, suffered was so that they could be in a position to bring the Philippian jailer to faith in Jesus Christ. One reason the jailer lost his dream of sound sleep and a secure jail was so he could have an opportunity to express faith in Jesus Christ.

God turned shattered dreams into something better, an encounter with Himself. Why does God allow bad things? Sometimes it is so He can do what He knows is best, blessing us with Himself.

A Shattered Marriage

Like every other young woman, Melanie got married with high hopes and big dreams. Yet her dreams of a happy life with Jim quickly unraveled, and too quickly they lay tattered in the dust of her tears.

Melanie found herself in the place she never imagined she

would be, a lawyer's office seeking a divorce. Hurt, angry, fed up, brokenhearted, and scared, Melanie sat down in front of the big desk. From the other side, the lawyer calmly listened to her story of lost love. When she finished, the lawyer calmly placed his notes in a big manila folder. With a confident smile, the lawyer looked Melanie in the eye.

"You do not need a divorce. You need Jesus."

The moment he said those words, a knife cut her heart and she knew he was right. For the next half hour, the lawyer shared with her the good news of the death, burial, and resurrection of Jesus Christ for her sins. With tears dropping off her cheeks, she bowed her head and gave her life to Christ. Her shattered dream led to her greatest joy. She met Jesus.

But that's not all. This story gets better. She went back to Jim and told him what had happened. He also gave his life to Christ.

Hold on. There's more. Jim and Melanie got involved in a good church. Soon Jim was called into full-time Christian ministry. Melanie's drunken, wayward husband became a loving man of God and a pastor. God used Melanie's shattered dreams to bring her to God, and then He gave her more than she had ever dreamed.

The Glorious Shattering of a Very Proud Man

At the age of thirty-eight, Chuck Colson arrogantly thought he had arrived. He had it all and didn't need God. As the chief counsel to the president of the United States, he wielded incredible power and had an ego to match. Thinking they could do no wrong, Richard Nixon's "hatchet man," Colson, among others, hatched a plan to steal secrets from their party's opposition.

Colson's big balloon burst as he and his cronies found themselves in a terrifying nightmare. Played out daily in the media was the sickening news of the dishonesty and petty political dirty tricks played by the Watergate Seven. Caught in the ugly web of the Watergate political scandal, his world crashed down around him as he found himself facing public scorn and ridicule, the loss of his lofty position, and a prison term.

This was the unbearably deepest, darkest time of his life. His dreams were shattered. His immense pride was broken. He was at the bottom and had nowhere else to look but up.

For the first time in his life, Colson thought seriously about a relationship with God. A concerned Christian pointed him to Christ. His failure and brokenness pointed out his need. Late one night he broke.

> *I was crying so hard it was like I was swimming underwater. . .then I prayed my first real prayer. "God I don't know how to find You, but I'm going to try! I'm not much the way I am, but somehow I want to give myself to You." I didn't know how to say it, so I repeated over and over the words:* Take me.[1]

When news of Colson's conversion to Christianity leaked to the press in 1973, the *Boston Globe* reported, "If Mr. Colson can repent of his sins, there just has to be hope for everybody."

Colson would agree. He admitted he was guilty of political "dirty tricks" and was blindly willing to do almost anything for the cause of his president and his party. Colson entered a guilty plea to Watergate-related charges. He entered prison as a new Christian and as the first member of the Nixon administration to be incarcerated for Watergate-related charges. He served seven months of a one- to three-year sentence.

Shortly after Colson was sentenced to prison, he wrote his testimony of coming to God in the best-selling book *Born Again*. After his release from jail, he founded Prison Fellowship Ministries to help meet the needs of the kind of men he had met in prison.

Colson experienced great pain and heartache that ultimately led to greater good for many, many others. Best of all, his hurt brought him to God.

Susan's Story

It began the morning after I defended my master's thesis, when I woke up with a pounding migraine, the stomach flu, and a cold. . . . It never went away. And for the next eight months, frustration grew as I battled chronic illness and fatigue. I had some good days, but mostly I was exhausted. I always seemed to have the flu, and my weight plunged from 125 to 92 pounds. Not long after, I was diagnosed with chronic fatigue syndrome (CFS), namely, permanent fatigue and a depressed immune system. . . .

When I couldn't work effectively, my self-esteem plummeted and depression soared. My relationships deteriorated because I was too tired to do anything and too angry to be near anyone—especially people who had the energy to lead a productive life. I could not function at the level I was accustomed to, and in my mind, if I couldn't do it all, I didn't want to live.

As a result, my heart became very dark. And my spirit screamed out to God—WHY? Why was I in such torment? If God had abandoned me to death, then let me die. But if I was meant to live, then heal me and let me function like a normal person.

For the first time in my life, I was unable to control my circumstances. And as I reached the end of my own strength, my only hope was to look outside myself for help—or something or someone who was much bigger than me.

Author and scholar C. S. Lewis says that pain is God's "megaphone to rouse a deaf world." It's true. I never looked to God much when I was healthy, successful, busy. . .able. I knew He was there, but it was only as I was stripped of all my resources that I really began to seek God and to cry out to Him from the depths of my heart.[2]

Shattered Dreams: Doorway to the Best Dream, God

As a counselor, Larry Crabb has spent a lifetime giving direction to good people trying to make sense of their shattered dreams. As a man, Larry has had to battle the brokenness that comes through losing a brother in a plane wreck, coping with cancer, and having a granddaughter with a life-threatening infection. Out of his experiences, he has learned some deep truths about shattered dreams.

> *Our shattered dreams never are random. They are always a piece of a larger puzzle, a chapter in a longer story. . .a necessary mile on the long journey of joy. . . .*
> *The suffering of shattered dreams must not be thought of as something to relieve if we can or endure if we must. It's an opportunity to be embraced, a chance to discover our desire for the highest blessing God wants to give us, an encounter with Himself.*[3]

In other words, one of the major reasons God allows suffering in our lives is to bless us with the greatest blessing He can give us—more of Himself. God allows our dreams to shatter so He can guide us to our unspoken but ultimate dream—a deeper, higher, more comprehensive, more pervasive experience of Himself. Crabb states, "Only when we want Him as we want nothing else will there develop in our hearts a space large enough for Him to fill."[4]

According to Crabb, our shattered dreams are God's unexpected path to joy and the school where we are forced to abandon every dream but the dream of truly knowing God. It is then that we experience the presence of God moving through every detail of our lives, both good and bad.

Why?

So why does God seem to stand idly by and allow His children to suffer? Because it is in the depths of sorrow that we finally look up and see. . .God.

Maybe you are broken by sorrow. Maybe you are suffering in pain. If nothing else, allow your brokenness to bring you to God. Do as Melanie or the Philippian jailer or Chuck Colson did. Believe on the Lord Jesus Christ and be saved. Cry out to Him. Ask Him to take your life.

If you already know God, maybe the reason you are suffering is to bring you to a deeper awareness of, appreciation of, and experience with God. Use your shattered dreams to draw more closely to Him than ever before.

Notes

1. Charles W. Colson, *Born Again* (Old Tappan, NJ: Revell, 1976), 116–17, emphasis his.
2. Susan Martinuk, "Why Me, God?" http://www.christianwomentoday.com/growth/susanmart.html (accessed November 11, 2006).
3. Larry Crabb, *Shattered Dreams: God's Unexpected Pathway to Joy* (Colorado Springs: WaterBrook, 2001), 4.
4. Ibid., 121.

11

To Stretch Us for Greater Growth
ROMANS 5:3-4

Are you suffering? Does affliction seem to come in waves that won't go away? Do you feel like it comes at you from all directions? Take hope. You are not alone. And you are not the first.

A devoted Christian man named Paul endured his own dizzying list of adversities. In fact, his sorrows are so numerous that he views himself as possibly the undisputed champion of pain. Read his testimony slowly, imagining how deeply these things must have hurt.

> *I've worked much harder, been jailed more often, beaten up more times than I can count, and at death's door time after time. I've been flogged five times with the Jews' thirty-nine lashes, beaten by Roman rods three times, pummeled with rocks once. I've been shipwrecked three times, and immersed in the open sea for a night and a day. In hard traveling year in and year out, I've had to ford rivers, fend off robbers, struggle with friends, struggle with foes. I've been at risk in the city, at risk in the country, endangered by desert sun and sea storm, and betrayed by those I thought were my brothers. I've known drudgery and hard labor, many a long and lonely night without sleep, many a missed meal, blasted by the cold, naked to the weather.*

> 2 CORINTHIANS 11:23–27 THE MESSAGE

Why would God allow such a good man to suffer so many bad things? In letters to his friends, Paul describes several benefits of suffering that we will discuss in coming chapters. One reason that especially stands out is his dogged insistence that in the hands of God, bad is good for us *because* it helps us grow. In fact, it is so good that Paul said he even shouted praises when he was surrounded by troubles!

> *There's more to come: We continue to shout our praise even when we're hemmed in with troubles, because we know how troubles can develop passionate patience in us, and how that patience in turn forges the tempered steel of virtue, keeping us alert for whatever God will do next. In alert expectancy such as this, we're never left feeling shortchanged. Quite the contrary—we can't round up enough containers to hold everything God generously pours into our lives through the Holy Spirit!*
> ROMANS 5:3–5 THE MESSAGE

Look at the benefits: "passionate patience," "the tempered steel of virtue," and "alert expectancy." Those three add up to personal spiritual growth.

Why do bad things happen to good people? Because in the hands of God, pain can help us grow and forge our character.

"What We Are Made Of"

It was Sunday morning, and thirteen-year-old Donald was getting dressed for church along with his father and his brothers. His mother was expected home any day from the hospital where she had successfully undergone surgery.

Feeling good and happy about life, Donald plopped a chocolate into his mouth. Then the telephone rang, and Donald heard his aunt tell his father the hospital wanted them to come right away. Somehow Donald knew what that meant: His mother was dead—from an embolism, he later learned.

Feeling sick, he rushed to the open window, lifted the screen, and let the chocolate fall from his mouth to the ground. Suddenly, his world was coming apart.[1]

After returning home from the hospital and facing the fact that his mother was gone, Donald gathered with his father and brothers in the dining room.

> *As we stood there with our arms around one another, crying our eyes out, my older brother, then in college, said, "Now we'll see what we are made of!" To this day, those words stand out as some of the most important words I have ever heard. When life comes apart, we have a lifetime opportunity to discover our inner qualities, our true strengths—"what we are made of," as my older brother put it—to let them come forth and allow them to grow.[2]*

What Donald discovered is that in the hand of God, difficulties become revealers of our character and aid in our development. He found that the path of progress runs through the valley of pain.

No Pain, No Pearl

As you know, pearls are some of the world's most beautiful jewels. They are naturally hard, yet incredibly smooth and perfectly round. As you may not know, they are the products of pain. Chuck Swindoll explains:

> *For an unknown reason the shell of the oyster gets cracked and an alien substance—a grain of sand— slips inside. On the entry of that foreign irritant, all the resources within the tiny, sensitive oyster rush to the spot and begin to release healing fluids that otherwise*

would have remained dormant. By and by the irritant
is covered and the wound is healed—by a pearl.[3]

A perfect, precious pearl is the product of a healed wound.
That is what makes a pearl so precious. Swindoll observed
that the tiny jewel was "conceived through irritation, born of
adversity, and nursed by adjustments."[4] Pearls can only be created
by suffering. Had there been no pain, there would be no pearl.
No wonder our heavenly home will have gates made of pearl.

No Wind, No Strength

A few months ago Cathy and I were shopping at an Amish
furniture shop. All the wooden pieces were wonderfully crafted
and beautiful. I noticed that most of the wood used was either
oak or pine. The oak was my first choice, until I looked at the
price tag. The oak was much more expensive than the pine. Why?

Both oak and pine trees can grow very large in size. Yet oak is
more coveted for furniture, floors, and outdoor use because oak is
harder, stronger, and more durable than pine. Because it is much
stronger, it allows header logs and floor beams to span greater
lengths.

Why is oak such strong wood? Oaks are noted for their
deep root systems. This allows them to face stiffer winds than
pines, which have a much shallower root system. When a big
storm comes along, the pines are vulnerable to being uprooted
and falling over, especially when they stand alone. However, the
deeper roots of the oak give it the ability to lean into the wind
and get stronger.

As we sink the roots of our spiritual lives deep into God and
His Word, God enables us to handle the storms of life. As we
withstand the winds of adversity, they serve to make us stronger.

No Wilderness, No Promised Land

> *There is no shortcut to wholeness: if you want to reach the
> Promised Land you must first go through the wilderness.*[5]

God promised a wonderful land to His chosen people, the freed
Hebrew slaves who escaped the tyranny of Egypt and Pharaoh.
But they could not simply leave Egypt and be in the Promised
Land. No. Instead, they had to first travel through the rugged
wilderness.

So it is with us. God promises us rich blessings, such as greater
power (2 Corinthians 12:7–10), deeper holiness (Hebrews 12:5–11),
and more fruit (John 15:1–8), but only after we have gone through
the wilderness of suffering. The wilderness is often dark, frequently
scary, and always difficult. But as Tim Hansel says, "The only way
out is through. It takes courage, tenacity, stamina, patience, God's
immense grace, and time. . .there is no such thing as an up without
a down."[6]

I don't know what wilderness you are facing, but I encourage
you to keep going through it, because the promised land waits on
the other side.

No Pain, No Gain

As that great weight lifter Benjamin Franklin once remarked,
"There is no gain without pain." Ronald Mehl, a pastor who
battled through cancer, wrote these words regarding the painful
times in our lives:

> *[They] always leave us with a list of things to clean
> up and fix up. They are when God restores to us the
> things we lose through negligence, ignorance, rebellion,
> or sin. For the Christian, [times of pain] are no-lose
> propositions. They help us see and acknowledge the
> loose shutters, missing shingles, and rotten fence posts*

*in our lives while returning us back to the One who
can make the necessary repairs.*[7]

We must not forget that God is a lot more interested in
our character than He is our comfort. He is willing to allow us
to experience difficulties in order to realize development. Our
heavenly Father is willing to let us fall down and skin our knees
a few times in order for us to learn to walk. He will let us go
through some pains so we can make some gains. Pastor, author,
and cancer survivor David Jeremiah has written:

> *We live in a skin-deep world. Our culture glorifies
> clothing, fashion, makeup, tummy tucks, and nose
> jobs. There is nothing wrong with any of those, but
> in the end they are only cosmetic. Character and
> substance are shaped in the crucible of adversity. Show
> me someone who lives a carefree life with no problems
> or trials or dark nights of the soul, and I'll show you a
> shallow person.*[8]

No Brokenness, No Wholeness

> *In pain, failure, and brokenness, God does His finest
> work in the lives of people.*[9]

God has an amazing way of using jagged, ugly, crushing
brokenness to develop deep and beautiful wholeness in the
lives of His people. I am not adequate to explain it, but I have
seen it spread through the pages of scripture and in the lives of
twenty-first-century people. We could start in Genesis with the
seemingly impossible dreams of Abraham and Joseph, go through
the wilderness with Moses, visit brokenhearted Hannah, run for
our lives with David, be taken captive with Daniel, and cry our
eyes out with Jeremiah. We could weep bitterly with Peter and be
knocked on our face with Paul. Alongside Mary, we could witness

the nightmare of the execution of her son Jesus.

Again and again, in every case, we would see the skillful hand of the Master Craftsman somehow using the worst of agonies to create amazing courage and character. Clay that cooperates with the potter is crafted into beautiful, useful pots.

Why?

So why does God allow bad things to happen to good people? One reason is that God will use the bad and the bitter to make us much better people.

Notes

1. Donald Morgan, *How to Get It Together When Your World Is Coming Apart* (Grand Rapids: Revell, 1988), 14.
2. Ibid., 17.
3. Charles Swindoll, *Growing Strong in the Seasons of Life* (Portland, OR: Multnomah, 1983), 164.
4. Ibid.
5. Clifton Burke, quoted in Tim Hansel, *Through the Wilderness of Loneliness* (Elgin, IL: Cook, 1991), 17.
6. Ibid., 17–18.
7. Ron Mehl, *Surprise Endings* (Portland, OR: Multnomah, 1993), 60.
8. David Jeremiah, *A Bend in the Road* (Nashville: W, 2000), 21.
9. Gordon MacDonald, *Rebuilding Your Broken World* (Nashville: Oliver Nelson, 1988), 28.

To Remind Us That We Are Not Home Yet

ROMANS 8

Slam!

My ear hurts. I just had an unethical tow truck driver call me a liar and hang up on me. This is the same man who charged me four hundred dollars more than he promised, yelled like a maniac at my wife and me, took my son's truck to his lot and impounded it without authorization, and then lied about the whole thing. I hate it when that happens.

Bad thoughts were starting to flood my mind. You know what I mean. First are the angry, crazy, *How can I blow up his office without getting caught?* type of thoughts. Then comes self-pity: *Why is this happening to me? What on earth did I do to deserve such unfair, unscrupulous, unrighteous treatment?*

Then I was struck with the profound thought: *Dave, you are writing a book called* 21 Reasons Bad Things Happen to Good People. *Which of the twenty-one reasons could this be?*

I thought of nearly a dozen possible, positive, probable products of this mess, but the one that best fit this situation is that bad stuff always reminds us that we are not home yet.

I recently had the joy of researching and writing a book on heaven. One of the plenteous reasons heaven is so heavenly is because there will be no irritations, injustice, price gouging, dishonesty, frustration, or need of tow trucks in heaven. Amen!

We make a grave mistake when we expect earth to be perfect and think of earth as our home. Neither is true. Life on earth is irritating, infuriating, frustrating, unfair, painful, and confusing.

Earth is a muddled mess; heaven is perfect. Earth is not our final forwarding address. Heaven is. We aren't home yet.

Life on the Cursed Planet

At the time of its creation, the earth was a lush, glorious, tropical garden paradise. All of creation—plants, animals, and humans—existed in perfect harmony under the rule of God. But because of the disobedience of Adam and Eve, planet Earth was placed under a curse. It has been groaning ever since.

> *To Adam he said, "Because you listened to your wife*
> *and ate from the tree about which I commanded you,*
> *'You must not eat of it,' cursed is the ground because of*
> *you; through painful toil you will eat of it all the days*
> *of your life. It will produce thorns and thistles for you,*
> *and you will eat the plants of the field. By the sweat of*
> *your brow you will eat your food until you return to*
> *the ground, since from it you were taken; for dust you*
> *are and to dust you will return."*
> GENESIS 3:17–19

At that moment, a dark shadow was cast over our planet. Thorns and other weeds began to grow (Genesis 3:18). Viruses were born. Plagues were hatched. Mosquitoes became bloodsuckers. Snakes became poisonous, as did some types of ivy. The table was set for the rise of killer storms, hurricanes, tornadoes, earthquakes, and droughts.

Since that fateful day in the Garden of Eden, creation has been groaning under the curse as it awaits the coming day of redemption. Paul writes:

> *I consider that our present sufferings are not worth*
> *comparing with the glory that will be revealed in us.*
> *The creation waits in eager expectation for the sons of*
> *God to be revealed. For the creation was subjected to*

> *frustration, not by its own choice, but by the will of the*
> *one who subjected it, in hope that the creation itself*
> *will be liberated from its bondage to decay and brought*
> *into the glorious freedom of the children of God. We*
> *know that the whole creation has been groaning as in*
> *the pains of childbirth right up to the present time.*
> ROMANS 8:18–22

Notice some of the ugly descriptions Paul chose to depict earth at this time: *sufferings, subjected, frustration, decay, groaning, pains*. But a better day, a brighter day is approaching. It will be a great day of *glory, liberation*, and *glorious freedom*.

Make no mistake. Sickness, sorrow, pain, problems, trouble, and turmoil have been commonplace on this planet since the curse. Sometimes we look for deep and complex reasons why bad things happen, when the easiest answer is that bad things happen because we live on a planet that is no longer truly good. Everything on earth is now stained and strained by imperfection. Even though earth is not as bad as it could be, it is no longer as good as it once was. When bad things happen, they remind us that we are not home yet.

Heaven, on Its Worst Day Is Far Better Than Earth on Its Best Day

One of the most comforting truths I discovered when I studied heaven—there are twenty-one amazing truths about heaven, by the way—is that heaven on its very worst day will be infinitely better than earth on its very best day.[1] This is true for many reasons. Consider this descriptive promise about heaven:

> *"He will wipe every tear from their eyes. There will be*
> *no more death or mourning or crying or pain, for the*
> *old order of things has passed away."*
> REVELATION 21:4

God will ultimately wipe away every tear. Death will be eradicated. There will be no more grieving. Having served its purpose, pain will be no more.

There Is No Sin in Heaven

In heaven there will be no sin or contamination created by sin's curse. This will make heaven so. . .heavenly. It will make it an amazingly wonderful home.

In heaven the transformational power of Jesus' death, burial, and resurrection for our sin will be experienced on a much greater level than we can now comprehend. Sin's power will be crushed, and its presence completely removed.

One definition of sin is breaking the law. In heaven no one will sin by breaking the law. In other words, there will be no bad people creating suffering for themselves or others in heaven (Revelation 21:8; 22:15). No one will rob, rape, or murder. No one will abuse, molest, assault, mug, or kidnap. You won't have to lock the doors. Security systems and fences will be unnecessary. Guns will be unnecessary, as will mace and pepper spray. In heaven, you won't be able to find courtrooms, jails, dungeons, or prisons, because there will be no criminals.

Sin is also defined as moral crookedness. Because sin will be absent in heaven, there will be no suffering caused by perversion, moral filth, or corruption. Pornography, prostitution, drug dealing, and sexual abuse will not exist there.

Because our sinful natures will not make the trip to heaven with us, we will not be the source of our own suffering. We won't ever put ourselves in pain because of our own sins, addictions, fears, guilt, shame, and regret.

There Is No Curse in Heaven

> *No longer will there be any curse.*
> REVELATION 22:3

Just as sin will be removed in heaven, its consequences will be absolutely absent (Revelation 22:3). The curse will be lifted. Imagine a world without any of the hardships caused as a result of natural disasters. Floods, storms, gales, tempests, tornadoes, typhoons, twisters, tsunamis, cyclones, whirlwinds, squalls, hurricanes, blizzards, whiteouts, blackouts, and monsoons will not exist. The land, air, and water will be perfectly pure. There will be absolutely no trace of pollution, smog, contamination, toxic waste, or trash. Cancer, famine, and drought will be forever gone. The environment will be pleasantly perfect in heaven. There will be no frostbite or sunburn.

In heaven, the human, plant, and animal kingdoms will live together in absolute harmony. Snakes won't tempt us to sin or be poisonous. Poison ivy won't itch, mosquitoes won't bite, and raccoons won't get in the trash (there won't be any). Termites won't eat your house. Bees won't sting. Dogs won't bite.

There will be no germs or viruses. You can cross all types of disease, illness, sickness, infirmity, infection, ailment, disorder, malady, and affliction off the list of potential sources of sorrow. No one will need a hospital, sanatorium, nursing home, rehab center, or clinic in heaven. Neither will there be morgues, funeral homes, or cemeteries. Heaven is all about life. Therefore, death, grief, and mourning will not exist (Revelation 21:4).

Why?

The joy of the Christmas season of 2004 was cruelly crushed under the giant waves of a killer tsunami, known by the scientific community as the Sumatra-Andaman earthquake. The devastating natural disaster began as an undersea quake that triggered a series of deadly tsunamis that spread throughout the Indian Ocean. Large numbers of people were killed and coastal communities across South and Southeast Asia, including parts of Indonesia, Sri Lanka, India, and Thailand, were inundated. The gruesome final tally lists more than 180,000 dead.

The response of Matthew Goh, a Malaysian architect and inventor, to the overwhelming devastation was like that of many others. He wrote on his Web site:

> *When the tsunami struck during Christmastime in the year 2004, I thought, Where was God? I was confused, sad, and even doubted if He existed, or if He really cared. Why, why, why. . .flooded my mind.*[2]

I know that there will be no tsunamis in heaven. We won't even need to ask, "Why?" again.

Heaven Is God's Final Answer to Pain and Suffering

While years, decades, or even a lifetime of suffering on earth may seem like an immense problem, such stands as a minute issue compared to the yawning length of eternity and the vast glory of heaven. Combine all the suffering of all the people on all of the planet through all of history, and it will register as less than a blip on the radar screen of eternal bliss. The bad times will be nothing compared to the good times. The pain will be forgotten because of the pleasure.

Because he understood this better than most, Paul was able to endure more suffering than most. No wonder he said:

> *I consider that our present sufferings are not worth comparing with the glory that will be revealed in us.*
> ROMANS 8:18

> *Therefore we do not lose heart. . . . For our light and momentary troubles are achieving for us an eternal glory that far outweighs them all. So we fix our eyes not on what is seen, but on what is unseen. For what is seen is temporary, but what is unseen is eternal.*
> 2 CORINTHIANS 4:16–18

We Are Not Home Yet

The familiar story is told of an elderly missionary couple coming home from years of faithful service on the mission field. They had served loyally, worked diligently, and sacrificed mightily. When they arrived back in the United States, their ship was greeted by a huge "Welcome Home" celebration. A band played, photographers jostled for pictures, dignitaries stood to offer an official welcome, brightly colored banners blew in the breeze.

The old missionary, Henry C. Morrison, smiled to himself as he thought, *Well, I guess it was not all unnoticed. This is beyond our wildest expectations.*

But when he and his wife disembarked from the ship, they were pushed aside in the rush to greet the real returning hero, Theodore Roosevelt, the president of the United States.

No one was there to greet the old couple. There was no banner with their name. No band to play a song. No dignitaries. Not a friendly smile, a hug, or even a welcoming word. Morrison gulped back the tears of his disappointment. Sadly he said, "I guess no one came to greet us."

"Don't be upset," he heard the Lord reply. "After all, you aren't home yet."[3]

Why?

So why do bad things happen to good people? One reason is to remind us that we aren't home yet.

Notes

1. If you are interested in heaven, you will want to read Dave Earley's *The 21 Most Amazing Truths About Heaven* (Uhrichsville, OH: Barbour, 2006).
2. Matthew Goh Kok Soon, *Asian Tsunami 2004,* http://www.matthewgoh.com/index.html (October 28, 2006).
3. R. Kent Hughes, *1001 Great Stories and Quotes* (Wheaton, IL: Tyndale House Publishers, 1998), 401.

13

To Shape Us More Like Jesus
ROMANS 8:28-29

Have you ever hurt so intensely that the pain was too deep for words? If so, you are certainly not alone. Most of us have been to that painful place where all we have is an awful, anguished inner groaning that reaches out to God for the tiniest ray of relief. Such is life on planet Earth. Such is life in the family of God.

The Christians who lived in Rome in the early years after the resurrection of Jesus were battling that type of cavernous brokenness. Historians tell us that to the general populous, Christians were viewed with suspicion, as *malefica* (the bringer of evil). Because they refused to give up their Christian identity and be swallowed by the pagan Roman culture, they were feared by Rome as dissidents who might upset Rome's hard-earned security. Under Claudius, emperor from AD 41 to 54, the Roman senate, in an official decree, declared Christians to be rebels and instigators. As such, they were considered as dangerous as an invasion by the barbarians. Since Rome's "universal peace" had been established by the ferocious efficiency of its army, Rome was willing to maintain it by whatever means deemed necessary, be it forced labor, exile, or even execution.[1]

This was the world Paul addressed in his letter to the Roman Christians. A catalog of their situation would include material suffering, physical affliction, vocational tribulation, family abandonment, and personal calamity. You can add persecution, hunger, homelessness, threats, backstabbing, other dangers, and even death.

These were good people. They loved God, followed Jesus,

and kept the faith no matter what. Why would a good God allow such very bad things to happen to such good people? The answer is found in a familiar passage and an overlooked truth.

Familiar Passage, Overlooked Truth

> *And we know that in all things God works for the good*
> *of those who love him, who have been called according*
> *to his purpose.*
> ROMANS 8:28

Most of us can quote Romans 8:28 by heart. It is one of the most encouraging promises ever pledged. The almighty God of the universe reassures His people that no matter what things happen, He works every single one of them for our good and His glory. Knowing and believing this enables Christians to live as "super victors" (Romans 8:37, my paraphrase). It binds us irrevocably to the love of Christ no matter what we face. No amount of trouble, trials, or tribulations; no hard times, hunger, homelessness, harshness, or hatred; no type of pain, pressure, or problem is so strong as to separate us from the love of God. Nothing is too complex, overwhelming, pervasive, or powerful to keep God from using it for good. God works all things for the good of those who are called according to His purpose. Wow!

Therefore, the question that must be answered when we are suffering is, "What is God's purpose?" Fortunately, we don't have to guess. The answer is in the very next verse.

> *For those God foreknew he also predestined to be*
> *conformed to the likeness of his Son.*
> ROMANS 8:29

In other words, God has known what He was doing all along. From the beginning, He decided to shape the character of those who love Him along the same lines as the character of His

Son. God knows exactly what He is doing, and He uses all the circumstances in the lives of His people, including the bad ones, to make us more like Jesus.

As I have already described, the apostle Paul was a veteran sufferer. Physical pain, emotional anguish, and spiritual torment were not foreign to his experience. While he learned many benefits of adversity, one of the greatest was that suffering is a familiar shaping tool in the hand of the Master.

The Master Sculptor

You must understand. It was not always a masterpiece. It was nothing more than a huge block of stone. Eventually, a sculptor named Agostino was contracted to turn it into a statue of the Old Testament hero David. He began preliminary efforts at shaping the legs, feet, and chest of the figure yet grew discouraged and ceased work. Then a man named Antonio was commissioned to take up where Agostino had left off. However, he botched the job and was soon terminated. The massive block of Tuscan marble looked worse than before as it remained forgotten and neglected for twenty-five years.

"The Giant," as the forsaken rock was churlishly called, lay exposed to the elements in the weeds outside the cathedral workshop. But a young artist named Michelangelo saw potential in it that no one else saw and begged for the commission. Receiving it, he spent the next three years hammering and chiseling away at the massive marble slab.

To Michelangelo, sculpture was the art of the "making of men." His approach to sculpture was to chip away the unnecessary pieces of stone in order to liberate the human body that was encased in the cold marble.[2]

Today his masterpiece, the *David*, stands alone as the most recognizable statue in the history of art. The sensational statue portrays the young man, David, at the moment he determined to go out and fight Goliath. Because of the masterful combination of size, shape, elegance, power, and motion, the *David* has become regarded as a symbol of both strength and youthful human beauty. The seventeen-foot marble statue stands as tall as a double-decker bus and weighs a staggering six tons. It is viewed by millions of visitors to Florence each year.

Stone turned to masterpiece. It took three years of the purposeful blows of a determined and gifted master to make marble take on the image of man. In a similar way, it takes a lifetime of enduring the hammer and chisel of God for Him to shape us into the image of His Son. Affliction is often painful and frequently confusing, but it is the way of the Master.

> *To be fanciful; if the hunk of stone out of which Michelangelo was hammering and chiseling his David could have spoken, it would no doubt have said it did not know what shape it was going to end up; it only knew that what was currently happening was painful. And to be realistic, that is often all we can say when God is using griefs and pains to sculpt our souls.*[3]

The story is told of a young boy who asked the master sculptor how he knew what parts of the stone to chisel off. The artist answered, "I take off everything that does not look like David."

What does God chisel from our lives through suffering? The short answer is that through our hardships He chisels off anything that keeps us from being like Jesus. What characteristics keep us from Christlikeness? They would include self-centeredness, selfishness, self-righteousness, self-sufficiency, and self-pity. There is also pride, arrogance, lust, greed, jealousy, envy, insensitivity, harshness, cruelty, apathy, and laziness. We could add dishonesty, deceitfulness, rebellion, idolatry, immorality, ignorance, bitterness, resentment, doubt, and fear. I left some off, but I think you get the idea. God's goal is for us to be more Christlike.

The Master Potter

> *This is the word that came to Jeremiah from the LORD:*
> *"Go down to the potter's house, and there I will give*
> *you my message." So I went down to the potter's house,*
> *and I saw him working at the wheel. But the pot he*
> *was shaping from the clay was marred in his hands;*
> *so the potter formed it into another pot, shaping it as*
> *seemed best to him.*
>
> > *Then the word of the LORD came to me: "O house of*
> *Israel, can I not do with you as this potter does?" declares*
> *the LORD. "Like clay in the hand of the potter, so are you*
> *in my hand, O house of Israel."*
>
> JEREMIAH 18:1–6

I enjoy art. I remember when one of my art teachers brought a potter's wheel to class. It was a big, round, flat wheel that spun around, powered by a small motor. If I close my eyes, I can smell the fresh clay. I feel the soft, smooth, wet clay in my hands. In my memory, I see the ugly, shapeless clay slowly taking shape as I mold it on the spinning wheel. I feel it spinning in my hands, gently rising under the pressure I put on it.

Clay has lumps in it. Those lumps don't just go away. They have to be worked out by the hands of the potter. This takes time. The more lumps the potter leaves, the less valuable the pot and the greater the odds of the pot cracking, or even blowing up, when it is fired in the furnace.

Spiritual clay has lumps. Those lumps don't just go away. They have to be worked out by the hands of the Potter. This takes time. The more lumps the Potter leaves, the less beautiful we become and the greater the odds of our cracking, or even blowing up, when we get fired by the intensity of extreme affliction.

After the potter has worked the clay, he or she fires it by placing it in a very hot kiln. The heat turns soft clay into a strong, useful pot.

The Potter lovingly works us in His hands as we spin on the wheel of life. He also fires us in the kiln of affliction. Thus, He makes us strong and beautiful. Thus, He makes us like His Son.

> *When in God's providence believers are exposed to the pressures of being isolated, opposed, tempted, humbled, disappointed, and hurt, the divine purpose is that these things should further our transformation into the likeness of our Savior.[4]*

God Shone All Over Her Face

Aunt Florence knew pain and restriction. She also radiated what it means to be transformed into the image of Jesus Christ. She is in heaven now, but a few years ago I described her with these words:

> *There she sat, day after day, tiny and crumpled, a prisoner to her wheelchair. Her limbs were withered and crooked, her joints gnarled and knotted by crippling rheumatoid arthritis. The joys and freedoms of daily life had long been taken from her. She could no longer take a walk across a field. She was unable to bend down and scoop up a wiggling grandchild in her arms. She could not cook her family a big meal. She could not even get up and clean her little farmhouse.*
>
> *Yet God shone all over her face.*
>
> *Even though she ached in continual pain, you would never know it by measuring her smile. If the frustrations of bondage to the chair or the bed bothered her, she never complained of it. Her heart was not filled with self-pity nor her countenance with sorrow. Resentment held no place in her heart. Instead, she sparkled with attractive depth of joy.*
>
> *She would literally light up when she spoke to*

*me of the wonderful preachers she saw on TV. She
peppered me with questions about the church that
was born in our basement. When she told me that she
prayed for me, I could tell she meant it and she had
and she did. Her Bible had that wonderful worn look.
Her clear blue eyes shone with that deep warmth of
someone who knew a secret.*

*God gave her the desire of her heart. All four of
her children grew up to live as committed Christians.
Her son became a minister and her daughters married
pastors. Her husband was a good and honest man,
rough through years of hard work, but he was always
so tender with her.*

*As I look back, it is so obvious now. Aunt Florence
had the Immanuel Factor. Her relationship with God
turned the potential prison of her wheelchair into
a sweet sanctuary of solitude. In spite of and in the
midst of her suffering, the glorious golden glow of God
shone all over her face and her life.[5]*

God used her suffering to shape her character and transform
her life. As she basked in His presence, the glory of His Son
shone from her life.

Why?

Why does a good God allow His children to experience bad
things? One of His primary purposes for pain is to shape us into
the image of His Son.

Notes

1. Teresio Bosco, "Persecutions of the Christians," http://www
   .catacombe.roma.it/en/ricerche/ricerca2.html (accessed November
   17, 2006).
2. Floria Parmiani, "Michelangelo's David," http://www.floria
   -publications.com/italy/italian_culture/michelangelo_david.html
   (November 17, 2006).
3. J. I. Packer, "Formed in the Wilderness," in *The Desert Experience:
   Personal Reflections on Finding God's Presence and Promise in Hard Times*
   (Nashville: Nelson, 2001), 112–13.
4. Ibid., 111–12.
5. Dave Earley, *Living in His Presence: The Immanuel Factor* (Minneapolis:
   Bethany House, 2005), 41–42.

14

To Remind Us That We Are the Body of Christ
1 Corinthians 12:12–14

On January 9, 2004, my good friend Joan Angus and her family experienced a horrible nightmare. Joan was pulling out in her minivan from a grocery store parking lot when her vehicle was hit by a semi that was going about thirty-five miles per hour. Joan was crushed by the heavy truck. Although Joan has no memory of her, a nurse passing the scene opened her airway so she could breathe.

> *I was. . .taken to Grant Medical Center. I had a broken hip and pelvis. I was suffering internal bleeding, so my spleen had to be removed. I was put in traction until I stabilized enough to have the hip and pelvis operated on. A few days later that was done. My hip has a plate that looks like a flattened chain that is screwed into the bone. It is at least ten inches long. I have another on the pelvis that is smaller.*

Joan also had a fractured skull and a traumatic brain injury, or TBI. Because of the TBI, she was unable to swallow properly, so a tube was put directly into her stomach to prevent aspiration—getting food, liquid, or medication into her lungs. Joan still has some symptoms caused by the TBI.

She has no memories of anything between the date of the accident and the middle of February. Once Joan was accepted into the Grant Rehabilitation program, twice a day she received physical, occupational, recreational, and speech therapy. In all, she spent sixty-three days in the hospital.

*It has been almost three years. I am as healed as I will
ever be. It is good enough. I am still somewhat numb
on my right side. I know I will never be the same
again. It makes me look forward to heaven even more
than I had before. I am going to run, skip, and jump
(which I can't do on earth anymore) to Jesus and thank
Him for all He has done for me. I can't wait!*

I will never forget going to the hospital on the night of Joan's
accident. When I arrived, there were already about two dozen
members of our church outside Joan's door praying and talking in
small groups. Joan's teenage daughters, Bethany and Jessica, were
repeatedly hugged and encouraged. We were afraid Joan could
not survive being crushed by the semi, and our hearts ached for
her stunned family.

When I was finally allowed to see her, I couldn't remember
ever seeing a human look less human. Blood, swelling, bandages,
tubes, and machines combined to create the macabre scene. As
I recall that night and try to write this chapter, I cannot help
choking back tears. As a pastor I have seen numerous people lying
in intensive care units, but Joan was probably the worst. I did not
see how she would live through it, and if she did, I was sure her
disabilities would ensure that she would never have a very high
quality of life.

Over the next few years, we saw God do many amazing
things for Joan and her family. I could use them as illustrations
for many of the principles discussed in this book. Her quiet
husband, Mark, rose to the occasion unlike few men I have ever
known. His confident faith in God and tender care for Joan and
the girls was a huge encouragement to me. He is not a public
speaker and never will be, but his e-mail updates on Joan's
progress were truly some of the greatest sermons I have ever
experienced.

Joan was incredibly restored to health, yet not fully. But her
faith-filled acceptance of the entire gruesome ordeal overwhelmed

me. She has often told me that she was glad she went into it knowing that sometimes bad things happen because we live in a no-longer-good world. I never heard her blame God or ask why. She continued to keep her wonderful sense of humor and to fight on.

But one of the most important benefits of the horribly bad things that happened to Joan and her family was not for them. It was for us. What was unbelievably bad for her was incredibly good for us. The body of Christ got to be just that for the Angus family.

> *My church acted as the hands and feet of Christ.*
> *My family received meals each night from January*
> *until my kids got out of school in June. My house was*
> *cleaned each week by teams of women from the church*
> *until I could manage it myself. I also had two women*
> *a day who sat with me once I came home. I could not*
> *be left alone because of the swallowing problem. This*
> *was such a huge amount of volunteerism, but I was*
> *never, ever made to feel like anybody minded the extra*
> *work.[1]*

The hospital chaplain was completely overwhelmed by the number of church members who came to the hospital to be with the family the night of Joan's accident. Other patients and their families were curious about a church that was so responsive to the needs of a hurting member.

I remember the first Sunday after the accident that Mark was able to come to church. People applauded him. I remember the first Sunday Joan was wheeled into church. People cheered, cried, and were incredibly happy to see her.

Christians who had been struggling with their faith were drawn back to Christ through the example of the Angus family. Church members who had never experienced the joy of selflessly serving others were blessed to help out. People beaten down by their problems were given new hope through the Angus family's valiant fight. I was going through a very dark season in my personal life, yet every time I got to speak with Joan, I was uplifted.

Such an awful, ugly, painfully bad event produced such deeply beautiful good things. Thank God!

The Beauty of the Body

The apostle Paul's most cherished description of the church is as the metaphor of the body of Christ. He was amazed by the potential unity of the body of Christ, saying, "The body is a unit, though it is made up of many parts; and though all its parts are many, they form one body. So it is with Christ" (1 Corinthians 12:12).

He loved the diversity of the body of Christ, writing, "Now the body is not made up of one part but of many" (1 Corinthians 12:14). He especially reveled in the value of each member:

> *If the foot should say, "Because I am not a hand, I do not belong to the body," it would not for that reason cease to be part of the body. And if the ear should say, "Because I am not an eye, I do not belong to the body," it would not for that reason cease to be part of the body. If the whole body were an eye, where would the sense of hearing be? If the whole body were an ear, where would the sense of smell be? But in fact God has arranged the parts in the body, every one of them, just as he wanted them to be. If they were all one part, where would the body be? As it is, there are many parts, but one body.*
>
> 1 CORINTHIANS 12:15–20

Of all the glorious similarities between the human body and the church of Jesus Christ, Paul stressed none more than the mutual dependency of each member of the body on every other part.

> *The eye cannot say to the hand, "I don't need you!"*
> *And the head cannot say to the feet, "I don't need you!"*
> *On the contrary, those parts of the body that seem to be*
> *weaker are indispensable, and the parts that we think*
> *are less honorable we treat with special honor. . . . But*
> *God has combined the members of the body and has*
> *given greater honor to the parts that lacked it, so that*
> *there should be no division in the body, but that its*
> *parts should have equal concern for each other. If one*
> *part suffers, every part suffers with it; if one part is*
> *honored, every part rejoices with it.*
>
> 1 CORINTHIANS 12:21–26

The eye needs the hand. The head cannot get along without the feet. Every part is interdependent on the others.

To summarize Paul's teaching: (1) We all are one, (2) we all are different, (3) we all are valuable, and (4) we all need each other. In a culture of individualism and increasing isolation, we need to be reminded that we need each other.

One thing that was flushed to the surface by Joan's accident was that Joan, Mark, and the girls needed each of us in very evident ways. Yet we needed them in possibly more important ways, as well.

We hurt when they hurt. We were thrilled when they made progress, because we are family, the family of God and the body of Christ.

Going It Alone Is Deadly

As a pastor for many years, I have seen numerous believers pull back from the church when trouble hits their lives. Some are embarrassed, some are distracted, and some are easily disappointed. The reason they don't participate in the body of Christ is not as important as that they decide to separate themselves. They feel hurt and choose to stay on the fringe "just until I heal."

But it doesn't work. Isolating oneself when hurt is exactly

the wrong way of thinking and responding. As a member of the body, we must be connected to the body to be fully healed. Let me explain.

Let's say that you had a chain saw get out of hand and accidentally cut off your finger. At this point you have two choices: Put the finger in your pocket and hope it heals, or speed to a surgeon and have it reattached as soon as possible. Which would you choose?

As you know, putting the finger in your pocket would condemn it to death. The life of the body flows from member to member through the bloodstream. If a finger is not connected to the life-giving blood flowing through the hand, it will turn black, rot, and die. However, if the finger can be reconnected, the body is amazingly equipped to heal the injured member in a miraculously small amount of time.

Healing in the Company of Friends

According to Dr. Nancy Burkhart, numerous medical and psychological studies show the healing power of going through suffering in the company of others.

> *Shearn et al. (1985) conducted a randomized study of men and women with rheumatoid arthritis and found that patients who participated in a mutual support group showed greater improvement in joint tenderness than a similar group of nonparticipants. This is also true for women with breast cancer who participated in a weekly support group. Spiegel et al. (1981) found that women with metastasis of breast cancer who participated in a weekly support group had significantly lower mood disturbances, fewer maladaptive coping responses, and fewer phobias than a similar control group. . . . Researchers have reported that just having one "significant" confidant can*

*improve overall health and well-being (Brown 1975,
et al., and Broadhead 1983, et al.).[2]*

Those in mutual support groups "showed greater
improvement." One significant confidant "improves health and
well-being." We need each other. Adversity is often the necessary
reminder that we are the body of Christ.

The first Christians faced incredible hardships, such as
ridicule, threats, losing property, beatings, and imprisonment.
Yet they endured these things because they went through them
together.

More Healing in the Company of Friends

One dark winter night, a drunken woman dressed in black
stepped out into the middle of the highway in front of Russ
Robinson's motor home, hoping to commit suicide. She lived,
but her bizarre act nearly killed Ron.

Yet he wrote that his connection to the body of Christ
through Christian friends saved him.

> *Their prayer support helped me begin the road to
> emotional recovery. . . . When I wrestled with God—
> seeking to make sense of the experience—people offered
> reassurance and other help. I needed people to pray
> with and for me, and I came to know what it was to
> have someone "weep with those who weep" (Romans
> 12:15 NRSV). I experienced how the body of Christ can
> extend real personal hands to someone in pain.[3]*

You can heal from any hurt and withstand immense pain
if you don't try to face it alone. You need a friend. You need a
family. You need a small group. You need a church.

Why?

Why does God allow suffering? One reason is that it often sparks His body, the church, into action and reminds us that we need each other.

Notes

1. Joan Angus's story is used by permission.
2. Nancy Burkhart, "The Value of Support Groups," Texas A&M University, University System Health Science Center, http://www.tambcd.edu/lichen/lifestyles/valuegroups/valuegroups.html (accessed March 28, 2007).
3. Bill Donahue and Russ Robinson, *Building a Church of Small Groups* (Grand Rapids: Zondervan, 2001), 39.

15

To Equip Us for Further Ministry
2 Corinthians 1:3-4

Think of me as a fellow-patient in the same hospital who, having been admitted a little earlier, could give some advice.[1]

The year I turned sixteen I had my summer well planned. I was going to take my driver's education courses, get my driver's license, and chase girls the rest of the summer. Just as summer began, however, I found myself doubled over with a severe stomachache. It kept getting worse, and I ended up in the hospital having my ruptured appendix removed. Because of the severity of the situation, I was in the hospital recovering for nearly a week and then was limited for several more weeks. While not totally torpedoing my plans, it was a severe setback.

As an immature teen, I wondered why God had let it happen at that time. Several years later, I got an answer.

I was a young pastor visiting a church member in the hospital. He was coming out of surgery and, after a short visit, went to sleep. The room he was in had two beds. In the other bed, lying uncomfortably, was a fifteen-year-old young man. I introduced myself and tried to chat with him. He seemed rather disinterested. Then I looked him in the eye and said, "I bet I can guess why you are in here."

"No, you can't," he replied, looking at me skeptically.

"Give me one guess," I said. He agreed.

"You just had an operation, and I am guessing that you had your appendix removed."

"How did you know that?" he asked.

"Easy," I said, "I can tell by the way you are lying in the bed." Then I lifted up my shirt to show him my appendectomy scar and the scar from when I had my spleen removed. "I got this scar when I was sixteen and this one when I was thirteen." He was impressed.

"So," he said and nodded, "you know just what I am feeling."

From then on, I had his attention. He opened up and told me all about himself. We had a great talk. Before I left, I had led him to Christ.

When I got in my car to leave the hospital parking garage, the thought hit me: So this is one good reason why I had appendicitis when I was sixteen.

The God of All Comfort

Called by many the greatest Christian of us all, Paul was a very good and godly man who was the veteran of extreme hardship. Persecuted for his faith, few have suffered as much. He faced frequent imprisonments, skin-shredding whippings, bloody beatings, shipwreck, betrayal, sleeplessness, hunger, cold, nakedness, and the awful stresses of leadership (2 Corinthians 11:23–29).

Why so much affliction for such a good and godly man? According to Paul, one of the lessons he learned in the school of severe sufferings was that the best person to help a sufferer is a veteran sufferer. Note what he said to some of his friends.

> *Praise be to the God and Father of our Lord Jesus*
> *Christ, the Father of compassion and the God of all*
> *comfort, who comforts us in all our troubles, so that we*
> *can comfort those in any trouble with the comfort we*
> *ourselves have received from God.*
>
> 2 Corinthians 1:3–4

Notice carefully what Paul wrote. We can paraphrase his words into three primary statements.

1. Our God is the Father of compassion and the God of all comfort.
2. When we suffer, our God comforts us.
3. God comforts us in our suffering *so that* we can comfort others in theirs.

When we suffer and learn to position ourselves to receive the comfort of God in our sorrow, we gain a priceless key that enables us to unlock hearts and minister to them more effectively. In a very real sense, suffering is a primary education and qualification for effective ministry. In commenting on this principle, one pastor wrote,

> *When a person has mastered the full curriculum of suffering—completed the course in dungeons and chains, in whips and scourgings, in shipwrecks and persecutions—then that person has received a master's degree in tribulation and is thoroughly qualified for the ministry of compassion.*[2]

Why did God allow such a good man as Paul to experience such horrible suffering? Why does God allow bad things to happen to good people? One reason is *so that* we will be better equipped to minister to others.

A Burden for Addicts

Recently, I was the guest speaker at a church in Pennsylvania. After the service, a woman named Bonnie told me her story. She had started smoking pot and drinking alcohol at the age of ten. She soon advanced to harder, intravenous drugs. For twenty years she had been bound by the painful, unrelenting chains of drug addiction, prostitution, and poverty.

Some caring Christian people had reached down, pulled her out of the gutter, and set her on the right path. They helped her discover real freedom in Christ. Clean for eight years, she now has a vibrant ministry to others who are breaking the chains of addiction.

"My heart is for the lowest of the low, the dregs of society, the hopeless and the helpless, because that's what I was," she said. "I want to help them just like someone else helped me. After all, who better to help an addict than an addict?" We could also ask, who better to help a sufferer than a sufferer?

Praying for Prodigals

You probably know of the world's most famous evangelist, Billy Graham. What you probably don't know is that two of his five children were spiritual wanderers and they broke their parents' hearts. Billy's wife, Ruth Bell Graham, used the pain she experienced as she prayed, watched, and waited for them to return to the fold to minister to others by writing a book titled *Prodigals and Those Who Love Them*.

Ruth's writing shows deep understanding of the confusion and fear of the ones who wait for their prodigals to return. The power of the book is the fact that she was writing from brokenhearted experience and practice, not theory. Because she had suffered the heartache of raising two prodigal children, she has the hard-earned credentials to minister to others with prodigals in their lives.

The Desert School of Ministry Training

Often we have a mistaken view of what qualifies us to minister effectively to others. Education is certainly helpful. Training is always good. Gifts are important. But we too often overlook the fact that it is in the loneliness of the wilderness and the difficulties of the desert that God truly prepares us to minister to others.

After enjoying the thrill of successful ministry, cohosting a popular television show, writing books, and speaking and singing to large audiences, Sheila Walsh fell apart and checked into a psychiatric hospital. She thought she checked in alone, but Jesus checked in with her. As she deeply experienced the love of God in her place of brokenness, He prepared her for much more effective ministry.

With deep understanding she writes, "You do not come out of the desert empty-handed but with a pocket full of gifts to share." One of the gifts she discovered in the desert was that she had a deeper, broader ministry than before. She says, "The amazing thing was my brokenness was a far greater bridge to others than my apparent wholeness had ever been."[3]

Looking back on the burdens and benefits of brokenheartedness, she wisely concludes, "I now believe that God delights to use those of us who have had our hearts and wills broken in the desert, who understand that if we stood in front of the Red Sea and it parted, we should get on our faces and worship, not call a press conference."[4]

"I Have Cerebral Palsy—What's Your Problem?"

The odds were cruelly stacked against young David. He was born with cerebral palsy, an incurable set of neurological disorders that permanently affect body movement and muscle coordination. When he was nine, his father died. The family home burned to the ground a few years later. His mother died from cancer when he was only fourteen.

Orphaned and shuffled from family to family, David had nowhere definite to call home. He lived with continual humiliation and ridicule from other kids. But he met Christ as a teenager. Through Christ, David triumphed over his tremendous hardships. In Christ, he discovered that he could be a victor instead of a victim.

Miraculously, God called him into a full-time ministry of evangelism, and in his early twenties, David began to hold nearly fifty revival crusades a year. Today he speaks to an average of one hundred thousand people a year in a variety of venues. He is married with four children.

I first heard him speak over twenty years ago and have never forgotten his message. At first, his slurred speech was irritating and difficult to understand. But like the rest of the audience, I was quickly captivated by his amazing story, positive attitude, and wonderful, self-deprecating sense of humor. He skillfully told his incredible story of overcoming such stiff odds. Then he looked at the audience and said, "I have cerebral palsy—what's your problem?"

All of our excuses for not serving God and all of our griping at our difficulties paled in comparison to what he had endured and still battles every day. His example of relying on Christ to rise above his overwhelming obstacles was an inspiration to all of us to rise above ours.[5]

A Broken Heart in Every Pew

"I know what it's like to sit in the pew with a broken heart," writes Ruth Graham, daughter of the famous evangelist Billy and his wife, Ruth Bell Graham.[6] With genuine candor and compassion, she tells her story in the book *In Every Pew Sits a Broken Heart*.

> *My own story is not tidy. Nor is it simple. My story is messy and complicated and still being written. I have known betrayal, divorce, depression, and the consequences of bad judgment. I have struggled to parent my children through crisis pregnancy, drug use, and an eating disorder. I have known heartbreak, desperation, fear, shame, and a profound sense of inadequacy. This is not the life I envisioned. Far from it.[7]*

Out of her pain, Ruth developed a deep desire to help others. With wisdom only gleaned in the classroom of suffering and sorrow, she discovered a ministry in helping the hurting.

> *My own plans for my life had been wrecked many times over, but it was not too late to join in on what God was doing. I knew I could serve others with compassion. . . . I was willing to touch hurting and broken people with the same grace God had shown me when I was hurting and broken.*[8]

Wounded Healers

In *The Wounded Healer*, Henri Nouwen argues that we heal from our wounds. He asks a profound question:

> *Who can take away suffering without entering into it? The great illusion of leadership is to think that others can be led out of the desert by someone who has never been there.*[9]

Through the empathy that comes from having been down the same road of suffering as another, we can minister more effectively than otherwise possible. Others can tell that we truly understand their pain and feel their hurt. A connection can be made. Trust can be built. Then real ministry can occur.

In describing the power of wounded healers, a young mother whose daughter died of sudden infant death syndrome shared:

> *It's as though people who have lost someone precious speak a different language. I don't have to explain things. There is a clear understanding that is so comforting.*[10]

Why?

So why does God allow bad things to happen to good people? One reason is that the very best person to help someone who is suffering is someone who has suffered. Let me encourage you to use your pain to more effectively minister to others.

Notes

1. In a letter from C. S. Lewis's to Sheldon Vanauken, April 22, 1953, quoted in *A Severe Mercy* (reprint, San Francisco, HarperSanFrancisco: 1987), 134.
2. D. James Kennedy, *Turn It into Gold* (Ann Arbor, MI: Vine, 1991), 34.
3. Sheila Walsh, "A Winter's Tale," in *The Desert Experience: Personal Reflections on Finding God's Presence and Promise in Hard Times* (Nashville: Nelson, 2001), 181.
4. Ibid., 179.
5. David Ring's full story is available on his Web site, http://www.davidring.org/biography.html (accessed March 28, 2007).
6. Ruth Bell Graham, *In Every Pew Sits a Broken Heart* (Grand Rapids: Zondervan, 2004), 12.
7. Ibid., 12–13.
8. Ibid., 168.
9. Henri Nouwen, *The Wounded Healer* (New York: Doubleday, 1979), 40.
10. Marcia Lattanzi-Licht, "Living with Loss: Bereaved Swim against Tide of Grief," 2001, Partnership for Caring, Inc., distributed by Knight Ridder/Tribune Information Services, http://itrs.scu.edu/fow/pages/Course/C-14.html (accessed March 28, 2007).

16

To Remove Our Self-Sufficiency

2 CORINTHIANS 12:5-10

Death by Fire

Converted at the age of eighteen, Dwight flung himself into Christian work a few years later. Highly energetic and fearless, the next decade became a whirlwind of spiritual progress and effective ministry. His Sunday school grew to a previously unprecedented size of fifteen hundred boys and girls, all from off the street, most coming to a life-changing relationship with Christ. When the nation went to Civil War, Dwight, as a leader of the Young Men's Christian Association, went to work as an evangelist, winning huge numbers of soldiers to Christ. Then he launched a Chicago church that rapidly grew in impact and size. He raised the funds and oversaw the creation of the first large, multipurpose YMCA building in America. He also helped develop unified Sunday school lessons that were soon taught by Sunday schools everywhere. All this time, he was out speaking around the country three or four days a week in large conferences and churches.

Outwardly, Dwight was a picture of spiritual power, yet he knew all of the activity was mostly the result of his own energy and zeal. He was financially broke, emotionally burned out, and spiritually bankrupt. He became deeply discouraged. Exhausted by his ministry treadmill, Dwight began to cry out to God for help. Once in a prayer meeting, he even broke down, rolling on the floor and groaning to God for spiritual power.[1] Days later an answer came to Dwight in an unexpected form. Sunday night,

October 8, as he finished preaching in his church, a fire alarm rang out. Droughtlike conditions and a strong wind quickly spread the fire across the city. Within minutes, flames engulfed huge sections of the town. The next morning a brokenhearted Dwight surveyed the damage. Four square miles of city were totally consumed, eighteen thousand buildings destroyed, one hundred thousand people left homeless, and over one thousand people dead. Destroyed in the fire was the new YMCA building, Dwight's church building, and his house. Later he stood with his wife and children, staring at the ashes that had once been their home. Ironically, nothing was salvageable except a tiny toy oven. Everything he had spent his life building was gone.

Insurance had not been held on any of the buildings, leaving nothing with which to rebuild. Dwight had to begin an exhausting campaign to raise funds to try and rebuild. He hated it, admitting, "My heart was not in the work of begging. I could not appeal. I was crying all the time that God would fill me with His Spirit."[2]

For Dwight, the anguish of his incredible loss stretched into an agonizing season of honest evaluation and numbing introspection. The purpose of the cross he was bearing is always one thing, and that is death, death to self. Dwight confessed:

> *God seemed to just be showing me myself. I found I*
> *was ambitious; I was not preaching for Christ, I was*
> *preaching for ambition. I found everything in my*
> *heart that ought not be there. For four months the*
> *wrestling went on within me. I was a miserable man.*[3]

Why did a good God allow such bad things to happen to such a good man and tireless servant? Sometimes God permits pain and suffering to strip us of our self-sufficiency. It is only then that we can realize His all-sufficiency.

A New Man

For Dwight, his incredible loss led to a rebirth of true spiritual power and truly effective ministry. Later he wrote, "After four months the anointing came." Describing it, he said, "Ah, what a day!—I cannot describe it, I seldom refer to it, it is almost too sacred an experience to name—Paul had an experience he never spoke of for fourteen years—I can only say God revealed Himself to me, and I had such an experience of His love that I had to ask Him to stay His hand."[4]

Dwight explained his experience to his friend D.W., who recorded it in his diary.

> *God blessed him with a conscious incoming to his*
> *soul of a presence and power of His Spirit such as he*
> *had never known before. His heart was broken by*
> *it. He spent much time just weeping before God, so*
> *overpowering was the sense of His goodness and love.*[5]

The change in Dwight was profound. In describing the new Dwight, one of his biographers wrote: "The quality of his relationship with God and his discernment of the difference between God's call and man's was so sharpened, and his power in ministry so enlarged that it sometimes seemed to him as if he had scarcely been—let alone useful—until this blessed time."[6] Such is the power of the resurrected life.

A New Power

Soon after this event, Dwight could not escape the sense that the Lord wanted him to spend some time in England resting, studying, and praying about his future. So he went and tried to hide on the sidelines. Eventually, however, he was recognized, and a pastor asked him to preach. Revival broke out in the church, and four hundred people made professions of faith during the ten days of impromptu meetings. Later he made the amazing discovery that Marianne Adlard, a bedridden girl, had literally prayed him over to England to be the tool of revival in her church. As a result, Dwight was given opportunity to be the tool of revival in many other English churches.

Dwight manifested the power of the resurrection in every association. A decade and a half before becoming president of the United States, Woodrow Wilson mentioned an unusual encounter in a barbershop when describing Dwight.

> *I became aware that a personality had entered the room and sat in the chair next to me. . . . I purposely lingered in the room after he left and noted the singular effect his visit had upon the barbers in that shop. They talked in undertones. They did not know his name, but they knew something had elevated their thought. And I felt that I left that place as I should have left a house of worship.*[7]

Dwight L. Moody returned home to Chicago a new man, and new ministry resulted. Orphanages, schools, ministry opportunities for women, and large crusades resulted. Most of his efforts still live and thrive today, 125 years later. They include Moody Press, the Moody Bible Institute, and Moody Church. Scholars estimate that in the pretelevision age, Moody preached the gospel to more than one hundred million people, and more than one million made professions of faith in Jesus Christ.

Why did a good God allow such bad things to happen to such a good man and tireless servant? Suffering removed his self-sufficiency and enabled Moody to experience what he truly wanted, the power of God's all-sufficiency.

Same Song, Second Verse

Dwight was not the first or last person who drank of the deep waters of devastating difficulties only to find a wellspring of real life and power. The apostle Paul gave this testimony:

> *I will not boast about myself, except about my weaknesses. . . . To keep me from becoming conceited because of these surpassingly great revelations, there was given me a thorn in my flesh, a messenger of Satan, to torment me. Three times I pleaded with the Lord to take it away from me. But he said to me, "My grace is sufficient for you, for my power is made perfect in weakness." Therefore I will boast all the more gladly about my weaknesses, so that Christ's power may rest on me. That is why, for Christ's sake, I delight in weaknesses, in insults, in hardships, in persecutions, in difficulties. For when I am weak, then I am strong.*
> 2 CORINTHIANS 12:5, 7–10

Paul was a high-octane guy. Prior to his encounter with Christ, he was a respected scholar, an influential, up-and-coming leader of Judaism, and a Roman citizen, as well. After meeting Christ, he became the voice of Christianity, a great church planter, a mighty missionary, and a powerful minister. Beyond that, his letters were considered the very words of God and were collected as scripture. Moreover, he was given amazing revelations of heaven and the future, unlike anyone before him.

Through it all, Paul was a scholar in the school of severe suffering. He faced hunger, homelessness, cruel criticisms, frequent imprisonments, physical beatings, spiritual attacks, and more. In suffering he learned many priceless lessons, including this: "When I am weak, then I am strong." His pain and weakness removed his pride and self-sufficiency so he could more fully experience God's strength.

In this passage, Paul mentions a source of frustration and torment neglected in his other catalogs of personal sufferings: "a thorn in my flesh, a messenger of Satan." For two millennia, scholars have debated the exact nature of this thorn in the flesh. Some think it was physical, in the form of chronic maladies, such as eye problems caused by a severe form of ophthalmia (Galatians 4:15), earaches, malaria, migraine headaches, epilepsy, or a speech disability. Others see it as an internal struggle coming in the form of incessant temptation. There are those who view the thorn as human in nature, caused by persistent persecutors or constant Christian critics. Some view the thorn as an emotional burden, such as depression. Some say it was spiritual assault, an actual messenger of Satan in demonic form.

So who's right? What was Paul's thorn?

We don't know.

I think it is intentionally unclear. Why? So no matter what your "thorn" is—physical, emotional, relational, spiritual, demonic, or whatever—you can still apply the principle that God's strength is made perfect in your weakness.

Paul considered this thorn a hindrance to wider or more effective ministry (Galatians 4:14–16), and he repeatedly petitioned God for its removal (2 Corinthians 12:8). Paul's language here suggests that this was probably the most intensive prayer struggle he ever faced.

And yet God said no three times.

Why?

It was through the continual torment of the constraining thorn that Paul was constantly reminded of the critical lesson anyone eager to be used of God must learn: "My grace is sufficient for you, for my power is made perfect in weakness."

As I study the lives of dozens of servants of God who were greatly used by Him, one common denominator links each: All have endured severe suffering. They all testify that their thorns were used to strip away their self-sufficiency and to bring them to a much deeper place of dependency on God.

Why?

So why does God allow bad things to happen to good people? Sometimes He wants to remove our self-sufficiency so we can really live His sufficiency; He reminds us of our abject weakness so we will fully rely on His amazing strength.

Notes

1. Sarah Cooke, *Wayside Sketches* (Grand Rapids: Shaw, 1895), 363.
2. D. L. Moody to C. H. McCormick, April 15, 1868, Moody Bible Institute archives.
3. Lyle W. Dorsett, *A Passion for Souls* (Chicago: Moody, 1997), 156.
4. A. P. Fitt, *The Life of D. L. Moody* (Chicago: Moody, n.d.), 65.
5. D. W. Whittle diary, quoted in James F. Findlay Jr., *Dwight L. Moody: American Evangelist, 1837–1899* (Chicago: University of Chicago Press, 1969), 132.
6. Dorsett, *Passion for Souls*, 159.
7. Woodrow Wilson, quoted in John McDowell, *What D. L. Moody Means to Me* (Northfield MA: Northfield Schools, 1937), 23.

To Expand Our Evangelistic Efforts

PHILIPPIANS 1:12–18

17

September 11, 2001

My friend Sujo John was born in Calcutta, India. He and his wife, Mary, arrived in the United States in February 2001. Only a few months after their arrival, Sujo and Mary secured employment in offices inside the World Trade Center. Wrestling with the call of God on his life, Sujo was at work on the eighty-first floor of the North Tower, or Tower 1, of the World Trade Center on September 11, 2001.

Sujo knew God was calling him to greater ministry, but he wasn't doing anything about it. He sent an e-mail to a friend at 8:05 a.m. from his office, telling him how he felt. At about 8:45 he heard a tremendous explosion, and the building shook and tilted. People were screaming.

American Airlines Flight 11, bound from Boston to Los Angeles with a full tank of fuel, had hit the floors directly above them. Debris from the aircraft flew into the office and flames erupted, consuming everything. Sujo and his coworkers looked down nearly ten floors through the huge crater in the floor.

Sujo's heart sank. He had no idea whether the plane had hit just their tower or the second tower, as well—the one where his wife worked. She was four months pregnant with their son.

I cannot imagine the thoughts that must have been running through his head and the fear that must have been gathering in his soul as they were evacuated through the stairway. His cell phone wasn't working, so he couldn't reach his wife.

When he looked out into the courtyard, he saw complete destruction. The fuselage of the plane, burning material, shattered glass, and bodies were strewn all over the courtyard. To Sujo, it looked like a war zone.

People were being led through different exits of the World Trade Center. Sujo decided to walk toward Tower 2 in hopes he might see his wife there. As he reached Tower 2, he heard a loud explosion, then all 110 stories of Tower 2 collapsed on those standing near the foot of the building—including Sujo.

> *Huge boulders and steel and mortar were tumbling down around us. We huddled at one end of the building, and I started praying for the blood of Jesus and asking God to give His strength. As I stared death in its face, I started having peace about this place called heaven. I told the people around me that all of us were going to die and if there was anyone who did not yet know Christ that they should call upon His name. At that point, everyone around me started crying: "Jesus!"*

Even in the midst of extreme tragedy, God was drawing people to Himself. Often, the most unlikely places and most inopportune times can be used of God to get out the message of the good news of Jesus.

Sujo's story continues: The whole building had collapsed, yet not a single piece of heavy debris had fallen on him.

> *I found myself in three feet of white soot. I got to my feet and was surrounded by silence. I could see dead bodies all around me. God directed me to a man on the ground who had a flashlight on him. I told him that only Jesus could save us and that we had to live. [When the man] stood up, I saw that the jacket he was wearing had "FBI" written on it. We held hands*

and started walking through the rubble. It was like a blizzard, one caused by all the concrete and ash that had been stirred up into the atmosphere.

The Holy Spirit then showed me a light flashing on top of an ambulance, so I told the man from the FBI that we had to head to that flashing light, since the ambulance was on the street. We somehow made it to the ambulance, which had been badly hit by flying debris. God kept the flashing light on top of the ambulance working to show me the way. From that point, it was relatively easy for us to make our way out.

In the midst of one of the greatest tragedies in American history, God was right there. He protected Sujo every step along the way. He joined the crowds that began running away from the skyscrapers to safer places. They ran and walked for an hour, and Sujo's cell phone still didn't work. Finally, at noon it rang. His wife was alive! Her subway train had reached its stop at the World Trade Center just five minutes after the first plane crashed, so Mary hadn't made it to work yet.

She told Sujo she had seen people jumping out of the burning buildings and that she had been hysterical, thinking he was dead. Eventually, they met at 39th Street in Manhattan near the ferry.

We looked back and could see both our buildings now only a pile of smoking rubble and ashes.

It is impossible to explain the sense of relief that flowed through us when we saw each other. Both of us had been so close to believing that we would never see each other again. When the explosion took place and the building was crumbling around me, images of my wife, parents, grandmother, and other loved ones flashed through my mind. The relief that we were alive was almost more than I could bear.

This story of ours is almost too good to be true. In spite of 110 floors of one of the tallest buildings in the world falling around me, I had not one single scratch on my body. For me this is proof that not only is God good, but that He knows the number of every single hair on our head. God never sleeps or dozes. This event proved to me that He is coming soon and that it is fundamentally important that we live every day as if He will be coming that very day.

I am reminded, however, that thousands died on this fateful day. We will all have to go one day. It was not our time to go that day. It is appointed for all men to die once. We are here to challenge the world with the question "Do you know where you are going?"[1]

Why did God allow Sujo to experience such a horrific nightmare? First, it gave him an opportunity to share Jesus with dying coworkers who desperately needed Him. Beyond that, it showed Sujo the miraculous power of God who delivered both he and his wife from death. But the most important outcome was that by looking death in the face and seeing people die all around him, Sujo recognized the call of God on his life. He was given an unquenchable burden and a flaming passion to go to the world with the question, "Do you know where you are going?"

Immediately following the tragic terrorist attacks of September 11, 2001, media from all over the world took interest in the powerful story of Sujo's miraculous deliverance. His story was featured in the *New York Times, Times-London,* CBC, *National Post,* BBC, "The 700 Club, Billy Graham Special," and TBN. Speaking opportunities poured in from all over North America. Because of experiencing the horrors of September 11, 2001, Sujo John was launched into full-time proclamation evangelism that has taken him to over four hundred cities in North America, Asia, and Europe and has resulted in the salvation of thousands.

Why do bad things happen to good people? Sometimes it is to expand the kingdom of God by creating greater evangelistic opportunities.

The Jailhouse Revival

The apostle Paul was imprisoned in Rome for his faith. Awaiting possible execution, he wrote a letter to his friends at a church in Greece.

> *Now I want you to know, brothers, that what has*
> *happened to me has really served to advance the gospel.*
> *As a result, it has become clear throughout the whole*
> *palace guard and to everyone else that I am in chains*
> *for Christ. Because of my chains, most of the brothers*
> *in the Lord have been encouraged to speak the word of*
> *God more courageously and fearlessly.*
> Philippians 1:12–14

Paul used his suffering as a means of sharing his faith. God knows that the best way to get the attention of a seeker is not necessarily by having His children live pain-free lives. One of the best ways to get the attention of sincere spiritual seekers is for them to see a Christian suffering triumphantly. Trials create the opportunity for testimony.

There were three groups of people who were evangelistically helped because Paul was in prison. Probably none of them would have been helped if he hadn't been imprisoned.

The first people who benefited from Paul's imprisonment were his guards. Paul was a major political prisoner. In the past, God had miraculously opened prison doors to set him free. The Romans were taking no chances, so Paul was in chains, probably chained to a Roman guard.

Picture this. When one guard would come on duty, Paul would tell him about Jesus and the guy might get saved. That guard would go off duty and another one would be chained to Paul. Paul would tell this guard about Jesus, and he might be converted. One by one the guards who were chained to Paul would end up giving their lives to Christ. Roman guards who never would have been exposed to the gospel any other way were converted to Christ because Paul was chained in prison. One man called it a spiritual chain reaction.

A second set of people positively impacted by Paul's imprisonment included the other Christian leaders. Because of the fierce persecution, most Christians were not as bold as Paul. But when they saw what Paul had the courage to do inside the prison, they got on board outside the prison. They became bold in telling others about Jesus outside the prison because Paul was bold inside the prison.

A third, and by far largest, group has benefited from Paul's prison suffering. You see, while Paul was in prison, the Philippians sent him a care package. He sent them a lengthy thank-you note that we now call the letter to the Philippians. They were blessed by Paul's prison epistle, and so have been millions of others across the centuries. This letter, Philippians, is one he might not have had reason or time to write if he had not been suffering in prison.

Much good came from the bad. The message of Christ was spread throughout the prison, around the area, and down through history. Wow!

Why?

So why do bad things happen to good people? What good can come from the bad? Maybe the reason you are suffering is to open up doors of testimony that would have been otherwise closed. Maybe your suffering will allow you to reach someone for Christ who might not be reached otherwise.

Note

1. Sujo John's story is used by permission. He is available for speaking opportunities and can be reached via his Web site, www.sujojohn.com, http://www.sujojohn.com/about_sujo_sept11.html (accessed March 28, 2007).

18

To Promote Us
to Greater Glory
PHILIPPIANS 1:21; PSALM 116:15

"Why? Why? Why did God allow this to happen?" the teenage girl sobbed, brokenhearted by her grandmother's death after a long, painful battle with cancer.

"Think of it this way," replied her wise pastor. "Look back to that last week of her life when she was suffering so severely. What if you had the power to take away all of her pain? If you had that power, would you use it?"

"Of course I would remove her pain," the young lady said.

"What if you also had the resources to send her on a deluxe vacation in a beautiful place with her close friends? Would you send her?"

"Yes," she replied.

"Let's also say that you could give her a brand-new body that would be much better than her old one ever was. Would you give it to her?"

"Yes."

"What if you could move her out of her little house in the bad neighborhood and set her up in a new house in a great neighborhood? Would you do it?"

"Yes," the girl said. "But you know I can't do all those things for her."

"That's true," the pastor replied. "But God can, and He did when He took your grandmother to heaven." He continued, "Your grandmother is on an eternal vacation. God has a brand-new body for her. She is in a place with no suffering or death. She is seeing friends and family members she hasn't seen in years.

She lives in a place especially designed for her, and it's in the best neighborhood on the planet."

"I see," she said. "So that's why God let Grandmother die."

"That's right," he said. "The death of someone we love is hard for us, but going to heaven is certainly good for them."

"But I'll miss her," she said.

"I know," he replied gently. "But remember, the years on earth in which we will miss our loved ones who have gone to heaven will go by quickly. They are next to nothing compared with eternity."

Graduation Day!

What is often seen as the very worst thing that can happen to a person—death—is actually a very, very good thing for God's people. For the Christian, death is not a termination, but rather a graduation to glory and a promotion to pure pleasure.

The first followers of Jesus believed the Bible taught that heaven is a genuine, literal, physical place. They always described heaven in concrete terms as a beautiful, wonderful, joyful, literal eternal home. Their confidence was obvious. For example, in AD 125 a non-Christian named Aristides wrote to a friend attempting to explain why the new religion called "Christianity" was so successful.

> *If any righteous man among the Christians passes from this world, they rejoice and offer thanks to God, and they escort his body with songs and thanksgiving as if he were setting from one place to another nearby.*[1]

For Christians, death is merely the door to the ultimate fulfillment of our dreams and destiny. When Christians die, they do not cease to live; rather, they start to live on a much higher level than any of us can possibly imagine.

Think about it. When Christians die, they don't pass away;

they go on ahead. They don't leave home; they go home. They don't pass on; they are promoted up. They do not leave the land of the living to enter the land of the dying. No. They leave the land of the dying to enter the land of the living.

I recently had the opportunity to study everything the Bible teaches about heaven.[2] I came away from that study thrilled with the glorious joy awaiting us in heaven. Some of the amazing truths I discovered about heaven include:

1. Heaven is a literal place, more real than anywhere you have ever been.
2. Heaven is the home you always wanted.
3. Heaven is the place of the best parties ever.
4. Heaven is the most exciting place in the universe.
5. Heaven, on its worst day, is better than earth on its best day.
6. Heaven is the home of the most, the biggest, and the best reunions imaginable.
7. Heaven is a world far greater than this one but far less than the one to come.
8. Paradise, or heaven, is a restored, purified, and perfected Garden of Eden.
9. Heaven will be the site of a wonderful awards banquet.
10. You can increase your capacity to enjoy heaven tomorrow by the choices you make today.
11. In heaven we will get a total body makeover.
12. Heaven will host the greatest wedding of them all.
13. Heaven will be a glorious kingdom ruled by King Jesus.
14. One day, heaven will have a glorious capital city.
15. Heaven is God's home.
16. Heaven will ultimately be a God-filled, pleasure-packed, fresh, thirst-quenching inheritance available to all who truly want to be there.
17. In heaven we will associate with amazing creatures called angels.

18. We will enjoy animals in heaven.
19. Heaven is a mind-expanding experience.
20. Heaven is the place where dreams come true.
21. Heaven is accessible from anywhere on earth through faith in Jesus Christ.

I Can't Lose!

Paul had lived a life full of thrilling adventure as he followed Jesus. Now he was old, tired, and ready for relief. His body ached from the beatings and hardships he had endured for Christ. Now locked in a prison because of his faith, he was smart enough to know that if he pushed the right buttons, he would be executed. That would end the persecution and the pain. He would get to go to a much better place.

Yet there were people on earth who still counted on him. They needed his leadership and teaching. So a dilemma developed. He was confident that with enough prayer support he could get out so he could help more people. But should he? Or should he press his point and find his neck on the executioner's block? Then he could go to enjoy heaven. In a letter to his friends, he described his dilemma and why he chose deliverance over death.

> And I'm going to keep that celebration going because I know how it's going to turn out. Through your faithful prayers and the generous response of the Spirit of Jesus Christ, everything he wants to do in and through me will be done. I can hardly wait to continue on my course. I don't expect to be embarrassed in the least. On the contrary, everything happening to me in this jail only serves to make Christ more accurately known, regardless of whether I live or die. They didn't shut me up; they gave me a pulpit! Alive, I'm Christ's messenger; dead, I'm his bounty. Life versus even more life! I can't lose.
> As long as I'm alive in this body, there is good

work for me to do. If I had to choose right now, I hardly know which I'd choose. Hard choice! The desire to break camp here and be with Christ is powerful. Some days I can think of nothing better. But most days, because of what you are going through, I am sure that it's better for me to stick it out here. So I plan to be around awhile, companion to you as your growth and joy in this life of trusting God continues.

PHILIPPIANS 1:19–26 THE MESSAGE

Notice the sentence at the end of that first paragraph: "Alive, I'm Christ's messenger; dead, I'm his bounty. Life versus even more life! I can't lose." What an unbeatable outlook on life. To continue to live was life. But to die was more life, eternal life, a higher quality of life. He could not lose!

Paul understood that for the believer, physical death is merely a step into eternal life. The "bad" of death is nullified by the "better" of heaven.

Saint Bert

My mom was a saint. I know that theologically all who have been born again are "saints" (see Philippians 1:1). At salvation we are "sainted" or "separated out" from this world to our God through faith in Jesus Christ. But my mom's sainthood was special. I am not saying that just because she was my mom. I am saying that because in the later years of her life, she so radiated the love of God that her pastor began to call her *Saint Bert*, and the nickname stuck.

Not long ago, after years of battling heavy physical afflictions, she quietly traded this life for the next. In preparing to speak at her memorial service, one verse quickly came to mind.

Precious in the sight of the LORD is the death of his saints.
PSALM 116:15

Mom's death was precious in the eyes of her Lord. This is because she, like all of us, was very valuable to Him because of the steep price He paid to redeem her. Her death was also precious because through her prayers, generosity, and loving acceptance of hurting people, she had become such a sweet and beloved person.

As a pastor, I have attended and participated in hundreds of funerals. There are but a handful I will never forget because it was obvious to me that the host of heaven had left heaven to join us in attendance. There seemed to be a golden glow in the room and the hint of angel music dancing in the air. The funeral was a glorious celebration of a wonderful, Christ-centered life and an anticipated arrival in heaven.

Why?

So why does God allow His people to experience the negative of death? Because He knows that death is the door to higher, greater, eternal life. It is a gift of blessed relief from pain and rest from labor. Even though we miss our loved ones who have gone ahead of us, we rejoice in the joy they have entered into.

Notes

1. Aristides, *The Apology of Aristides the Philosopher*, 15, http://www.early christianwritings.com/text/aristides-kay.html (accessed September 20, 2006).
2. See Dave Earley, *The 21 Most Amazing Truths about Heaven* (Uhrichsville, OH: Barbour, 2006).

19

To Give Us Further Instruction
HEBREWS 12; PSALM 119:67, 71

When C. S. Lewis was between the tender ages of six and eight, his mother suffered and died. As a young man, Lewis fought in World War I, where he faced the horrors of seeing friends grotesquely wounded and killed. As an adult, he pursued a relationship with his emotionally distant father, to no avail. Later in life, he fell hopelessly in love with an unlikely woman. She was a divorced, former communist atheist, who had recently become a Christian. Her name was Joy. She became the joy of his life. A popular movie was made of their courtship and marriage called *Shadowlands*.

Early in their marriage, Joy developed cancer. A few years later, she died. Out of his sorrow, Lewis developed a deeper appreciation of some of the costly benefits of pain and grief. One was the ability of agony to get our attention. With deep wisdom he wrote, "Pain is God's megaphone to rouse a deaf world."[1]

Why does God allow bad things to crowd into the lives of good people? One reason is that in pain we learn to hear God's voice. As one observed, "It is where we are wounded that God speaks to us."[2]

In Pain We Learn to Hear God's Voice

Steve was a good father, husband, and Christian. He also was a highly successful commercial Realtor who lost his company when the economy went south. Out of work and out of options, he heard God's voice through the megaphone of his pain. Adversity taught Steve many valuable lessons.

I began to see that my walk with Him had gradually eroded during years of fruitfulness. With the blinder removed from my eyes, I began to see myself in an unattractive new light; God was showing me hard truths about myself that I didn't want to see. Such things as my reputation, the esteem of my colleagues, and my net worth and assets had become pagan idols in my life. . . .

These things all came as a shock because I thought I had it all together. God was "lovingly beating me up". . . . These were difficult lessons to learn, but I sat at His feet and listened to His Word. And in the midst of the discipline, I came to love Him more than I had in the past—much more.[3]

Nancie also was a student in the school of suffering. Her story is that she was the model pastor's wife, publisher, mother, and church member. Yet bad things began to pile up on her. Nancie found herself numbly enduring the loss of her parents, the challenges of raising five children, one of whom had special needs, chronic pain, exhausting fatigue, paralyzing depression, and a dizzying schedule. She felt completely incapable of managing the overdesigned, overbusy, draining life she had created for herself.

When breakdown forced her to confront her pain, she learned many lessons. One of the most important was to listen to God. She writes, "I learned that the desert is not a tragedy. The tragedy is to fail to hear what God was saying to me there."[4]

In Pain We Learn Lessons in the School of Suffering

The first-century Roman world was a faith-draining world for a Jewish Christian. Read slowly from Hebrews 10:32–34; 11:35–38 the roll call of pain the Hebrew Christians had to endure that could only be called "a great contest and conflict of sufferings."

- Being made a public spectacle through reproaches and tribulations
- Seeing friends and loved ones endure the same
- Enduring the seizure of property
- Being tortured and refusing to be released
- Facing jeers and flogging
- Being chained and put in prison
- Being destitute, persecuted, and mistreated
- Finding shelter only in deserts, mountains, caves, and holes in the ground
- Facing death by stoning, being sawed in two, or being beheaded by the sword
- Having nothing to wear but sheepskins and goatskins

My hardships seem small compared to what they endured. It was to these people who were living in the school of suffering that God said, don't throw away your faith (Hebrews 10:35), keep running the marathon of faith (12:1), and focus your eyes on Jesus (vv. 2-3).

I often need to be reminded that most of life is education, not destination. One of the primary agents of instruction is adversity. There is much to be learned in the academy of agony. Sometimes the purpose is teaching us a truth, an attitude, or even a skill that we did not previously know. Often the objective is to correct our thinking, attitudes, or behavior.

Chapter 12 of the letter to the Hebrews addresses the matter of education through adversity. The author reminds us of several lessons we can learn when the storms of life grow intense.

1. *Don't feel sorry for yourself. You are not the only one who is suffering.*

> *In this all-out match against sin, others have suffered far worse than you, to say nothing of what Jesus went through—all that bloodshed! So don't feel sorry for yourselves.*
> HEBREWS 12:4 THE MESSAGE

Suffering has a way of isolating us from contact with others. We often feel as if we are the only one or that the extent of our suffering is much greater than others. Not true. Every human faces hardship. Adversity is the atmosphere of humanity.

2. ***Don't blow off the lessons or, on the other hand, be crushed by suffering. Parental discipline is part of family life. The fact that God brings discipline into our lives proves that we are His children.***

> *Or have you forgotten how good parents treat children, and that God regards you as his children? "My dear child, don't shrug off God's discipline, but don't be crushed by it either. It's the child he loves that he disciplines; the child he embraces, he also corrects."*
> HEBREWS 12:5–6 THE MESSAGE

When my boys were small, they occasionally (okay, frequently) needed some discipline. We jokingly referred to administering the "board of education to the seat of understanding."

Our neighbor boys loved to be at our house and feel like part of the family. One day I caught them all in the backyard hiding behind the shed gambling with cards and poker chips.

As I gathered up my sons to discipline them, the neighbor boys asked, "What about us?"

"I only discipline my sons," I said. "It's up to your father to discipline you."

One reason I know I am the child of God is because He does not let me get away with much. If He did not love me so much, He would not discipline me so severely. Suffering is not a sign that my heavenly Father does not love me; it is evidence that He does.

3. *Don't quit. Discipline is part of God's parenting process.*

> *God is educating you; that's why you must never drop out. He's treating you as dear children.*
> HEBREWS 12:7 THE MESSAGE

Once, when my son Andrew got in trouble I found him in his room packing up his bags to run away. He was about four or five years old at the time. I asked him why he was leaving, and he told me it was because I was too mean. Today both he and I are glad he didn't run away. After a few years of going through the struggles of growing up, he has become a wonderful Christian young man, and we have a very close relationship.

I am coming to understand that most of my years on earth will be spent in the school of suffering. This is not because God does not love me, but because He does and He is preparing me for a close relationship with Him throughout eternity.

4. *Don't view what you are experiencing as punishment. It is training.*

> *God is educating you. . . . This trouble you're in isn't punishment; it's training, the normal experience of children.*
> HEBREWS 12:7–8 THE MESSAGE

One of the encouragements I have gained in researching and writing this book is that I have been reminded that every Christian goes through periods of discipline and difficulty. No believer is immune. No one is beyond the need of the Father's loving instruction.

5. *Embrace God's training.*

> *Only irresponsible parents leave children to fend for themselves. Would you prefer an irresponsible God? We respect our own parents for training and not spoiling us, so why not embrace God's training so we can truly live?*
> HEBREWS 12:9 THE MESSAGE

Real growth occurs when we move beyond numbly enduring suffering to the point of actually embracing it. I have to confess that even when I do try to welcome hardship, I struggle to maintain that outlook. But, as we have seen throughout this book, God produces many positive blessings in our life through affliction. As long as we remember that, we can embrace His training process.

6. *Don't get discouraged. Maintain the big perspective.*

> *While we were children, our parents did what seemed best to them. But God is doing what is best for us, training us to live God's holy best. At the time, discipline isn't much fun. It always feels like it's going against the grain. Later, of course, it pays off handsomely, for it's the well-trained who find themselves mature in their relationship with God.*
> HEBREWS 12:10–11 THE MESSAGE

If we look at our current difficulty, it can be discouraging. But present pain plays an important role in a larger, longer process of producing maturity in our lives. Look at the ultimate rewards instead of the existing sorrows.

7. *Don't go it alone.*

> *So don't sit around on your hands! No more dragging
> your feet! Clear the path for long-distance runners so no
> one will trip and fall, so no one will step in a hole and
> sprain an ankle. Help each other out. And run for it!*
> HEBREWS 12:12–13 THE MESSAGE

Suffering will shrink your world. The drudgery of dealing with
daily difficulty and suffering can cause you to circle the wagons
too tightly and focus on you and yours completely. One day you
will wake up on a tiny, lonely island. Paradoxically, often the best
way to lighten your load is to help carry someone else's burdens
for a while.

My mom battled persistent respiratory challenges, tremors,
macular degeneration, and arthritis, along with depression and
other issues. Yet she was able to go on and remain contagiously
positive in spite of it all. One of her secrets was that she found
tremendous joy and relief in helping others. Visiting people in
the hospital, taking flowers to shut-ins, and giving money to
struggling young couples were some of her keys to being a victor
over her difficulties.

In Pain We Learn to Live God's Word

One of the greatest Bible scholars and teachers in history, Martin
Luther, said, "Affliction is the best book in my library."[5] Another,
Charles Spurgeon, said, "Very little is to be learned without
affliction. If we would be scholars, we must be sufferers."[6]

We all have a tendency to get off track, especially when it
comes to the ways of God.

> *Before I was afflicted I went astray, but now I obey
> your word.*
> PSALM 119:67

It was good for me to be afflicted so that I might learn your decrees.

PSALM 119:71

Corrie ten Boom was thrown into a horrendous German concentration camp because of her faith in Christ. With an aching body, an empty stomach, and freezing hands, she wrote these words from her lice-infested bed: "We are in God's training school and learning much."[7]

My friend John Thomas writes, "The real truths of scripture cannot be completely grasped in a classroom setting. They are discovered and only fully understood in the laboratory of life."[8] He's right.

Why?

So why does God allow bad things to storm the gates of good people? Often it is merely part of the parenting process, designed to teach us how to practically live out the truths of God's Word.

Notes

1. C. S. Lewis, *The Problem of Pain* (New York: Macmillan, 1940), 93.
2. W. H. Auden, quoted in *The Desert Experience: Personal Reflections on Finding God's Presence and Promise in Hard Times* (Nashville: Nelson, 2001), 72.
3. Quoted in David Jeremiah, *A Bend in the Road* (Nashville: W, 2000), 128–29.
4. Nancie Carmichael, "The Gift of the Desert," in *The Desert Experience: Personal Reflections on Finding God's Presence and Promise in Hard Times* (Nashville: Nelson, 2001), 78.
5. Martin Luther, quoted by Elizabeth Skoglund, *Coping* (Ventura, CA: Regal, 1971), 23.
6. Charles Haddon Spurgeon, *The Treasury of David*, vol. 6, Psalms 119–124 (Grand Rapids: Baker, 1981), 166.
7. Corrie ten Boom, *Clippings from My Notebook* (Minneapolis: World Wide, 1982), 56.
8. John Thomas and Gary Habermas, *Why Me?* unpublished manuscript, 112.

20

To Call Us to Increased Prayer
JAMES 1:5

I am a dad. I have three sons named Luke (sixteen), Andrew (eighteen), and Daniel (twenty). The older ones are in college. I think each of them would tell you that I have a very good relationship with them, but. . .when everything is going great, they don't call me much. If I call them, they are happy to talk. But they are busy, and they don't need me.

However, let them face some adversity they think I can help them with, and they are quick to call. Why?

They call because they need me.

I am happy to hear from them and glad to help.

It's not that they're bad guys. They aren't. Actually, they are great young men. It's not that they are selfish, unloving, uncaring brats—not at all. It's just that they are normal young men.

Let me ask you a question.

When do you talk to your heavenly Father most frequently?

Many of us would argue that prayer is a very important activity. Yet the vast majority of us would admit that we don't pray as much as we would like.

When do you pray most often?

Do you pray more when everything is going great or when everything is going wrong?

I thought so.

We usually pray most when times are tough.

Why? Because it is when times are tough that we realize how desperately we need God.

Why does a good God allow His children to face bad things?

One reason is that privation, pressure, pain, and problems can prompt us closer to Him through prayer. We seek Him for provision, direction, and help.

Who Ya Gonna Call?

The pastor of the first church in the world, Pastor James, and his congregation of Hebrew Christians were good people who faced a plethora of problems. They dealt with severe opposition and persecution (Hebrews 10:32–34). Many were publicly exposed to insult and persecution. Some had their property confiscated. Others were imprisoned. Some of their leaders were killed for their faith (Acts 8, 12). In his profound statement about the benefits of facing trials, James recommended that his readers add increased prayer to the list.

> *Consider it pure joy, my brothers, whenever you face*
> *trials of many kinds, because you know that the testing*
> *of your faith develops perseverance. Perseverance*
> *must finish its work so that you may be mature and*
> *complete, not lacking anything. If any of you lacks*
> *wisdom, he should ask God, who gives generously to all*
> *without finding fault, and it will be given to him.*
> JAMES 1:2–5

"He should ask God." Suffering can be confusing. We wonder: *Why me? Why now? When will it get better? What do I do now? Which way do we turn? Who do we tell what? Who can help me through this?*

James tells us that when we are suffering and are not sure what to do, we need to call on God. God wants to help us. He will give us the wisdom we need.

David: A Prayer for Every Problem

David's life was both thrilling and excruciating. He knew lofty highs, but he also experienced devastating lows. Falsely accused, nearly murdered, hunted like a fugitive, hiding for his life in a desert wilderness, he experienced his share of problems. Plus, he had numerous battles with the barbaric Philistine armies. Added to those adversities were the agonies caused by his sins. Public ridicule, the death of a child, and bone-aching guilt and shame were heartbreaks he brought on himself. Family problems nearly destroyed him. One of his daughters was raped by his son. Another son grew resentful and rebellious, launched a successful political coup that kicked David off his throne, and was later tragically killed. What a massive, miserable mess!

Out of the volume of his life and sorrows, David wrote more than seventy-five songs. Many are biographical, reading like journal entries. A significant number were prayers, or better, pleadings with God written from the depths of his difficulties. David was called "a man after God's own heart" in part because he persistently turned his problems into prayer. His psalms teach us there is a prayer for every problem. For example, when he began to run for his life from crazed King Saul and his troops, David turned to God and prayed.

> *Save me, O God, by your name; vindicate me by your might. Hear my prayer, O God; listen to the words of my mouth. Strangers are attacking me; ruthless men seek my life—men without regard for God. Surely God is my help; the Lord is the one who sustains me.*
> PSALM 54:1–4

> *O my Strength, I watch for you; you, O God, are my fortress.*
> PSALM 59:9

In a humiliating turn of events while running from Saul, David had to fake insanity to keep from being killed by the Philistines. The great warrior had to become the drooling village idiot. This problem was turned into prayer. Later he wrote of his deliverance.

> *I sought the LORD, and he answered me; he delivered*
> *me from all my fears. Those who look to him are*
> *radiant; their faces are never covered with shame. This*
> *poor man called, and the LORD heard him; he saved*
> *him out of all his troubles. . . . The eyes of the LORD*
> *are on the righteous and his ears are attentive to their*
> *cry. . . . A righteous man may have many troubles, but*
> *the LORD delivers him from them all.*
>
> PSALM 34:4–6, 15, 19

Cries from the Cave

At one point, with Saul and his army breathing down David's neck, he was forced to hide out in a cave. That's right—a dark, dank, dirty cave. Maybe you feel as though you are in a cave of hardship. Noted English author and preacher Charles Spurgeon observed, "Caves make good closets for prayer."[1] Turn your cave into your prayer closet. David did.

David did not come to God with polite, memorized words or impressive eloquence. David's despair and dire circumstances invoked in him a deep inner wailing. He *cried out* to God. It has been said that the best style of prayer is that which cannot be called anything else but a cry.

I figure that if the pain is so severe that I'm going to cry anyway, I may as well cry out to God. David knew what it meant to cry out to God. Listen to the confident cries and pleading prayers for help he offered God from the cave.

> *I cry out to God Most High, to God, who fulfills his*
> *purpose for me. He sends from heaven and saves me,*

> *rebuking those who hotly pursue me; God sends his*
> *love and his faithfulness.*
> PSALM 57:2–3

> *I cry aloud to the LORD; I lift up my voice to the LORD*
> *for mercy. I pour out my complaint before him; before*
> *him I tell my trouble. . . . I cry to you, O LORD; I*
> *say, "You are my refuge, my portion in the land of the*
> *living." Listen to my cry, for I am in desperate need.*
> PSALM 142:1–2; 5–6

His hard times were not immediately relieved. David lived the lonely life of a fugitive for many difficult desert years. His career was shot, his reputation marred, his family removed. He was homeless and, at times, hopeless. The sad emptiness of the sparse wilderness must have evoked images of better days and bred a deep longing in his soul. In his pain, at night, alone in the desert wilderness, he cried out to God. Hear the anguish in his prayers.

> *O God, you are my God, earnestly I seek you; my soul*
> *thirsts for you, my body longs for you, in a dry and*
> *weary land where there is no water.*
> PSALM 63:1

When the ugly ordeal with Saul was finally finished, David gazed back on his years of hardship and marveled at God's response to his prayers. Triumphantly he testified of God's rescue. Read carefully his powerfully poetic imagery.

> *I love you, O LORD, my strength. The LORD is my rock,*
> *my fortress and my deliverer; my God is my rock, in*
> *whom I take refuge. He is my shield and the horn of*
> *my salvation, my stronghold. I call to the LORD, who is*
> *worthy of praise, and I am saved from my enemies.*
> PSALM 18:1–3

*The cords of death entangled me; the torrents of
destruction overwhelmed me. The cords of the grave
coiled around me; the snares of death confronted me.
In my distress I called to the LORD; I cried to my God
for help. From his temple he heard my voice; my cry
came before him, into his ears.*

PSALM 18:4–6

*He reached down from on high and took hold of me;
he drew me out of deep waters. He rescued me from my
powerful enemy, from my foes, who were too strong for
me. They confronted me in the day of my disaster, but
the LORD was my support. He brought me out into a
spacious place; he rescued me because he delighted in me.*

PSALM 18:16–19

Never Far from the Need to Pray

After David finally became king, his problems did not
disappear; they merely took different forms. Again he turned
his problems into prayer. For example, when confronted about
his adulterous sin, he longingly pleaded for cleansing. Out of
a broken and repentant heart he wrote the classic Fifty-first
Psalm.

*Have mercy on me, O God, according to your
unfailing love; according to your great compassion blot
out my transgressions. Wash away all my iniquity and
cleanse me from my sin. . . . Cleanse me with hyssop,
and I will be clean; wash me, and I will be whiter
than snow. Let me hear joy and gladness; let the bones
you have crushed rejoice. Hide your face from my sins
and blot out all my iniquity.*

PSALM 51:1–2, 7–9

One of the most heartbreaking seasons of David's life was when his son Absalom turned against him and took the throne from him. It was an ugly, nasty, vile affair. I can't imagine how deeply it must have hurt him to have his own son repudiate everything about him and rebel so cunningly and violently. I can only guess at the pain he felt when he had to flee his throne because his people had turned against him. Yet confidently David prayed.

> O LORD, how many are my foes! How many rise up against me! Many are saying of me, "God will not deliver him." But you are a shield around me, O LORD; you bestow glory on me and lift up my head. To the LORD I cry aloud, and he answers me from his holy hill.
> PSALM 3:1–4

> I lie down and sleep; I wake again, because the LORD sustains me. I will not fear the tens of thousands drawn up against me on every side.
> PSALM 3:5–6

Turn Your Problems into Prayer

David was not the only one who allowed pain to press him to God in prayer. The secret to the success of people like Moses, Hannah, Asa, Hezekiah, Elijah, Nehemiah, Mary, Peter, Daniel, and Paul was that they learned to turn problems into prayer. We must do the same. Maybe you want to read back through the prayers of David highlighted in this chapter and make some of them your prayers. Use them to cry out to God.

Why?

What good can come from the bad things that we face? Our problems prompt us to draw closer to our heavenly Father in prayer.

Note

1.   Charles Haddon Spurgeon, *The Treasury of David*, vol. 7 (Byron Center, MI: Associated Publishers and Authors, 1970), 7:293.

21

To Refine Our Faith
1 PETER 1:6–9

Tested by Fire

When he awoke on that Thanksgiving Day morning, Merrill Womach was a handsome, vibrant man actively engaged in his expanding Christian music business and singing career. Yet by early afternoon, his life took on a devastating new direction as his plane crashed in a sea of flames. Amazingly, as the EMTs were pulling him from the fiery wreck and loading him onto a stretcher, he began singing praise to God!

Graciously, God spared his eyesight and vocal chords through the horrible fire and the numerous surgeries. Miraculously, his voice actually grew richer and fuller than before.

But Merrill's hands and head had been charred black and bloody by the furious flames of the fateful plane crash. His once handsome face was horribly disfigured and scarred. All his features had been consumed by the flames. His physical pain was drawn out, intense, and agonizing. But his emotional pain was much greater. Imagine how crushed he felt when he overheard his nurse say to an orderly, "Have you seen that horrible-looking creature? I can hardly touch him."[1] Think of how his wife, Virginia, must have felt to see nothing but a black charcoal blob where her husband's face had been.

Over the next fourteen years, Merrill somehow endured more than fifty excruciating skin-graft operations. Skin was taken from the non-charred parts of his body and sown onto the burned sections. Recovery from such operations was long, frustrating, and intensely painful.

By day there were painful treatments. At night he faced frightening nightmares of burning alive or being thrown into an oven or having his skin cut off with a machete. Understandably, he feared drug addiction to pain killers, and he battled severe seasons of loneliness, fear, and depression.

When he could finally go out in public, he was greeted by stares, laughs, fear, and insults. One woman actually yelled, "Hey clown, take off your mask. It isn't Halloween yet."[2] Obviously, the fire severely tested Merrill's and Virginia's faith. Resolutely, they persevered, believing God had put them through the ordeal for a purpose. Virginia wrote:

> *Although it sounds strange, I feel it is an honor that God chose us. God had a purpose in all our suffering, and I believe it is to share the strength we have gained from it with others who have suffered or who will suffer tragedy in their lives.[3]*

Merrill said:

> *"God has tested us through the fire. And out of the suffering He was making something beautiful in our lives."[4]*

Why did God allow that good man to go through that awful fire? Why did his wife have to face such a trying ordeal? Often God uses the fire of affliction to mold character, refine faith, and make something more beautiful of our lives.

The Night of Regret!

I imagine it to be a night Peter would never forget and always regret. Unusually warm in Jerusalem for the spring, the heat was soon turned up on high. After an emotional meal, Jesus had led His disciples into the garden at Gethsemane for a time of rest and prayer. Jesus seemed strangely and unnecessarily energized, intense, serious, and agitated. But Peter had a hard time staying awake.

Then the reason for Jesus' mood became abundantly clear. Loud, angry voices and bright torchlights jolted him from drowsiness. The next thing Peter knew, Jesus was arrested and dragged off.

With hot adrenaline heightening his senses, Peter followed at a distance to find out what was going on—big mistake. The Sanhedrin was hot. Jesus had gone too far. Obviously Jesus was deep in very hot water, and a firestorm was coming down that had the power to engulf them all.

Fear began to pump through his veins and flow down his spine like boiling water. He was sweating. Thoughts floated through his head like angry bursts of steam.

What was going to happen to Jesus? These people wanted to kill Him.

What was to become of their movement of radical truth and love? The authorities wanted it squelched.

What about him? What was going to happen to him, Jesus' right-hand man, the one with the big sword and the big mouth? If they were going to kill Jesus, what were they going to do to him?

Fear gave way to doubt.

Was Jesus really the Messiah? Was He really the only way to God?

Was following Jesus worth the suffering Peter was about to face? What did he really believe about Jesus and about God?

Before he realized what had happened, he heard himself denying Jesus Christ not just once, but *three* times.

Immediately, he could not fathom what he had done. The fearless follower had given in to fear and had lost his faith. How could he have done it? He knew Jesus was real. This was one of the few times Jesus had ever needed him, and he had failed. Boy, had he failed.

Why did Peter give up and give in? He was so ashamed—excruciatingly shamed. He could never look at himself in the mirror again. The pain of regret was overwhelming. Brokenhearted, he put his head in his hands and sobbed.

The Day of Rejoicing!

Then came a day Peter would never forget and always rejoice over. Thousands of people were gathered in the temple courts because of the Pentecost celebration. With unusual boldness and fearless faith, Peter proudly, passionately, powerfully proclaimed the glories of the resurrected Lord Jesus Christ. They could stone him; they could crucify him. It did not matter. His faith was greater than anything they could do. Jesus was alive! He had risen from the dead! He would tell the world, no matter what it cost.

The crowd was inspired and deeply impressed by Peter's faith-filled words. They had the authoritative weight of the Word of God. The multitude accepted Peter's words, they believed them, and they were willing to obey. It was amazing. Three thousand people were willing to throw in with Jesus and be baptized in water—because of Peter and his words.

The Refining of Your Faith

It was with a clear eye and deep experience that thirty years later Peter was able to pen more faith-building words. His words were designed to encourage and educate people who were facing severe sufferings and painful persecutions because of their faith in Jesus Christ. They were good people who were trying to survive in a life full of trouble. Why were they experiencing such tough times?

Peter addressed that question. He did not sugarcoat the trials, but he did applaud their benefits. Read Peter's words carefully.

> In this you greatly rejoice, though now for a little while you may have had to suffer grief in all kinds of trials. These have come so that your faith—of greater worth than gold, which perishes even though refined by fire—may be proved genuine and may result in praise, glory and honor when Jesus Christ is revealed. Though you have not seen him, you love him; and even though

> *you do not see him now, you believe in him and are*
> *filled with an inexpressible and glorious joy, for you*
> *are receiving the goal of your faith, the salvation of*
> *your souls.*
> 1 PETER 1:6–9

Rejoicing in trials? A faith more valuable than gold? Refined by fire? What was Peter talking about?

Refined by Fire

Gold is a very precious metal. Its sparkling character, beautiful hue, malleable makeup, and unique metallurgical properties—including resistance to tarnishing and corrosion and virtual indestructibility—have made gold one of the world's most coveted precious metals since early history. Ancient Egyptian, Minoan, Assyrian, and Etruscan artists produced elaborate gold artifacts as early as 3000 BC. As increasingly complex economic systems developed, gold was used as a high-denomination currency and eventually as a backing for paper currency systems.

Yet when it is mined, gold is not in a pure state. Naturally occurring gold is dispersed throughout the earth's crust and is usually combined with other elements, such as silver, copper, platinum, and palladium. In order to isolate pure gold, a refining process must occur.

Gold is smelted by skilled craftsmen using intense heat. Fire separates the gold and silver from the dross impurities. The furnace is heated to extremely high temperatures. Gold melts at 1,062 degrees Celsius or 1,943 degrees Fahrenheit; therefore, it is smelted at temperatures above that. Refining is a practice that must be done precisely and methodically to ensure the full recovery of gold and to produce an end product that is free of impurities.

Goldsmiths heat the gold ore in a furnace. As they do, the impurities separate from the gold, and they skim them off. This takes time, as not all of the impurities were dislodged at once; different ones are only revealed as the temperature increases. After the appropriate amount of heat and subsequent removal of impurities, the final product is beautiful, pure gold.

What Peter is saying in his first letter is that he has learned that we can actually find joy in our trials *because* they can be used by God to refine our faith. While pure gold is highly valuable in this life, pure faith is much more valuable in both this life and especially in the next. Such faith can be refined only in the furnace of affliction.

The intense heat of severe suffering separates our pure faith in God from the dross of our trust in other things. Trust in material things, other people, and ourselves proves insufficient in the heat of intense trials. Only pure faith in God will get us through.

The Refiner, the Crucible, the Fire, and the Gold

Amy Carmichael lived a challenging life of selfless dedication and total abandonment to the Savior. She had one purpose: to make God's love known to those trapped in utter darkness. As a young woman, she obeyed the call of God and went to Dohnavur, India, where she served fifty-six years as a missionary, never taking a furlough.

Amy knew hardship. Living as a single female missionary in India at the end of the nineteenth century was very difficult. This was compounded by her calling to save children who had been sold into slavery by their families to be used as Hindu temple prostitutes. Once rescued, these children needed to be cared for, fed, housed, and educated. Her organization, Dohnavur Fellowship, ministered to hundreds of these children at a time.

Later in life, Amy experienced a horrific fall that left her an invalid for the remaining twenty years of her life. Amy, a gifted author, spent the time of her confinement writing many of her thirty-five beautiful books, including *Candles in the Dark*; *Edges of His Ways*; *God's Missionary*; *His Thoughts Said. . .His Father Said*;

Thou Givest. . .They Gather; If; and *Toward Jerusalem.* In *Gold by Moonlight* she tells of her experience with the refiner's fire.

> One day we took the children to see a goldsmith refine gold after the ancient manner of the East. He was sitting beside his little charcoal-fire. . .the goldsmith never leaves his crucible once it is on the fire. . . .
>
> In [the crucible] was the medicine made of salt, tamarind fruit, and burnt brick-dust, and embedded in it was the gold. The medicine does its appointed work on the gold, "then the fire eats it," and the goldsmith lifts the gold out with a pair of tongs, lets it cool, rubs it between his fingers, and if not satisfied puts it back again in fresh medicine.
>
> This time he blows the fire hotter than it was before, and each time he puts the gold into the crucible the heat of the fire is increased: "It could not bear it so hot at first, but it can bear it now; what would have destroyed it then helps it now."
>
> "How do you know when the gold is purified?" we asked him, and he answered, "When I can see my face in it, then it is pure."[5]

God the Goldsmith

God is the Master Goldsmith of our faith. He wisely uses the heat of affliction to produce the pure gold of genuine trust in Him. Carefully He heats the furnace, allowing impurities in our faith to be separated from the real thing. These are skimmed off, revealing a pure faith. Beloved Bible teacher Warren Wiersbe wisely observed:

> *When God permits His children to go through the*
> *furnace, He keeps His eye on the clock and His hand*
> *on the thermostat. His loving heart knows how much*
> *and how long (1 Peter 1:6–7).*[6]

God the Goldsmith knows just the right amount of the heat of suffering He will allow in order to purify our faith. He knows exactly how long to allow our hardship to continue to make our faith more than "as good as gold." He will continue the process until He can see His reflection in the purity of our faith.

Why?

So why does a good God allow bad things to happen to good people? Sometimes the intense heat of suffering is a refiner's fire, purifying the gold of godly faith, forging the steel of godly character.

Notes

1. Merrill and Virginia Womach with Mel and Lyla White, *Tested by Fire* (Grand Rapids: Revell, 1976), 29.
2. Ibid., 104.
3. Ibid., 123.
4. Ibid., dustcover.
5. Amy Carmichael, *Gold by Moonlight* (Fort Washington, PA: Christian Literature Crusade, n.d.), 36, emphasis added.
6. Warren Wiersbe, quoted in David Jeremiah, *A Bend in the Road* (Nashville: W, 2000), 5.

Final Thoughts

What to Do When Bad Things Happen to You

Bad things will happen to good people. But God is powerful, wise, loving, and gracious, and He can use negatives to produce plenty of positives.

One of the central lessons of Christianity is this: *The real issue is not what happens to me so much as what happens in me.* Bad things will happen to you. The big question is: How will you respond to them?

As we have seen, one of the most profound stories of bad things happening to a good person is the story of Job. Job was one of the most moral, righteous, loving men on earth, yet in a rapid series of events, he lost everything—his wealth, his health, and his children. We can learn several valuable lessons from Job concerning how a good person should respond to bad things.

Job Faced His Affliction. . .

1. *With the choice to worship—Job 1:20–21*

> At this, [the news that all his flocks, herds, servants, and his ten children had been killed] Job got up and tore his robe and shaved his head. Then he fell to the ground in worship and said: "Naked I came from my mother's womb, and naked I will depart. The LORD gave and the LORD has taken away; may the name of the LORD be praised."
>
> JOB 1:20–21

Job faced his affliction with worship. The word here translated as "worship" means he put his face on the ground in humble submission to God. He said, "The LORD gives, the LORD takes away." He worshipped Jehovah as the One ordering his life, who is ever worthy of praise whether in His infinite wisdom He gives or takes away. Then he said, "The name of the LORD be praised." The word *praise* means to "speak highly of." Even though things were not going well for Job, God had not changed. He was still worthy of praise.

Let's learn a priceless lesson from Job: *Our response is always our choice.* We cannot control what happens to us, but we can control *how we respond to* what happens to us. We make the choice. When bad things come, how will you choose to respond? With praise and worship? Or with pouting and whining? Will you be God-focused or self-focused?

Job made his choice. He decided to praise and worship God. He got on his face and said, "The name of the LORD be praised." God is worthy even when life is rotten. God is worth it, even when life hurts badly. Real worship can be painful and costly.

2. *Without a sense of entitlement—Job 1:21; 2:9–10*

> *His wife said to him, "Are you still holding on to your integrity? Curse God and die!" He replied, "You are talking like a foolish woman. Shall we accept good from God, and not trouble?" In all this, Job did not sin in what he said.*
> JOB 2:9–10

Soon after losing everything, poor Job woke up covered from head to toe with painful, oozing, angry, red boils. His not-so-encouraging wife said, "Why don't you curse God and die?" But Job refused.

Job faced his affliction without a sense of entitlement. His attitude was, *I came with nothing. I will leave with nothing. What I have in between is up to God. It's God's choice. Sometimes He chooses to give, and He has given me much. Sometimes He chooses to take away. What right do I have to complain?*

Notice that he did not say what we so often are tempted to say. He did not say, "It's not fair. I have my rights. I deserve better than this. I am entitled to a pain-free, problem-free life."

No, he looked at his grief-stricken wife and said, "Shall we accept good and not trouble?" Job did not expect to live a pain-free, trouble-free life. He understood that life is not easy. It's not comfortable. It's hard. It's painful. Sometimes it really hurts. He accepted the reality without a sense of entitlement.

3. *Without sinning, losing his integrity, or cursing God— Job 1:22; 2:3, 9*

> *In all this, Job did not sin by charging God with wrongdoing.*
> Job 1:22 (emphasis added)

Sometimes we see suffering as justification for sin. We think it is not fair; it is not right, so we have a perfectly good excuse to sin. Yet Job faced tremendous affliction without sinning. He did not allow anything, even the worst of things, to become an excuse to sin.

> *Then the LORD said to Satan, "Have you considered my servant Job? There is no one on earth like him; he is blameless and upright, a man who fears God and shuns evil. And he still maintains his integrity, though you incited me against him to ruin him without any reason."*
> Job 2:3

> *His wife said to him, "Are you still holding on to your integrity?"*
> Job 2:9

What is integrity? The Hebrew word speaks of wholeness, entireness, uprightness, innocence, sincerity. In Genesis 20:5 it is rendered as "a clear conscience and clean hands." It is used in Psalms as a synonym for righteousness and blamelessness.

Job was blameless before the disasters happened, and he was blameless afterward. Trials did not change him for the worse. He did not get bitter. If anything, he got better.

Satan had hoped he would curse God to His face (Job 1:11). But Job gave him no such satisfaction. To Job, God was worthy of following even when his life was in ruins. Think about it. Which God is better? A God who allows only good things or a God worth trusting even when bad things happen?

4. *Refusing to give up on life or on God—Job 2:9–10; 13:15*

> *Though he slay me, yet will I hope in him.*
> JOB 13:15

The suicide rate in the U.S. has skyrocketed. While twenty thousand Americans are murdered each year, thirty-one thousand take their own lives.[1] Part of this, no doubt, is the result of being a culture that does not know how to deal with pain. From our earliest years, we hear commercials telling us that we have a right to have our pain relieved. So when the type of pain hits that will not go away with a pill, we have a hard time dealing with it. When affliction hits, it is natural to want to give up.

Pain can cause us to want to quit on life. But Job did not follow his wife's advice to give up and die.

He wished he had not been born, but he did not wish himself dead or try to kill himself. He had several "good excuses" to take his life. He had lost all his wealth. All his kids had died. He was in excruciating pain. His wife encouraged him to die. Later in the book of Job, his friends tell him that all his suffering is his own fault. No one on earth gives him any encouragement to go on. On top of that, God is purposely silent. Yet Job refuses to quit on life. That is how good people are to face bad things—with a refusal to quit on life.

Even more impressively, Job did not quit on God. He did not follow the intent of Satan, which was to press him to get bitter toward God. He refused to give up on God. He had a faith that went beyond the good things and carried him through the bad. He did not believe *because of* circumstances. He believed *in spite of* circumstances. As we saw in chapter 2, this type of faith can shut Satan's mouth.

Think about it. He believed with a lot less information than we have. He had no Bible to read; it had not been written. He could not gain comfort from the book of Job. And the church did not exist then. Nevertheless, he stayed faithful. Do you realize what this shouts to us? If he could do it, so can we! We can be faithful. We can hang in there. We can go on.

5. *With questions—Job 3:11; 7:20; 21:7*

> *"Why did I not perish at birth, and die as I came from the womb?"*
> JOB 3:11

> *"If I have sinned, what have I done to you, O watcher of men? Why have you made me your target? Have I become a burden to you?"*
> JOB 7:20

> *"Why do the wicked live on, growing old and increasing in power?"*
> JOB 21:7

A myth running through Christianity says that good Christians don't question God. Not so. The presence or absence of questions does not reveal the level of our faith. Real faith wrestles through questions. And in the face of pain, it is normal to ask questions.

If we asked no questions, we would not be human. We would be mere robots. God does not mind us asking questions. His person and past history can stand up to our questions.

6. *With genuine grief—Job 3:1; 6:1–3*

> *Then Job replied: "If only my anguish could be weighed and all my misery be placed on the scales! It would surely outweigh the sand of the seas—no wonder my words have been impetuous."*
> Job 6:1–3

The reason Job's response to affliction is so compelling is because he was no robot. He was flesh and blood, a human being with feelings and emotions. This man lost his wealth, his career, his employees, and his businesses. His children were killed. His health was gone. He was in constant physical pain. So what did he do? He did what any human being must do—he grieved.

Job suffered victoriously, but he did not suffer without grief. This is another of those hurtful Christian myths: Strong Christians do not grieve. That is untrue, as grief is a natural expression of humanity. *Being a Christian does not make me less of a human. It makes me more of one.* Failing to grieve is a mistake.

When I counsel with families who have lost loved ones, I encourage them to grieve. They should go ahead and allow themselves to feel common emotions that come from loss. They need to work through the inevitable sense of shock and denial and the feelings of anger and guilt. They need to acknowledge the numbing sensation of loss.

7. *With prayer for others—Job 42:10*

I have read several books about Job, and they miss what I consider to be one of the biggest keys to this book. When you read Job, you read of his loss of wealth, health, and family. You read of his grief and questions, his meeting with God, and finally, of his release from the flames of affliction. When you read that section, be sure that you do not overlook verse 10.

> *After Job had prayed for his friends, the LORD made him prosperous again and gave him twice as much as he had before.*
> JOB 42:10

God did not free Job from his pain and bless him with twice as much *until* he changed his focus from himself to others and prayed for his friends. Suffering has an ugly way of making us extremely self-centered. Life keeps closing in until all we can see is our problems and our pain. This must not be allowed to continue. Yes, we need to vent our frustrations, and yes, we need to grieve. But before too long, we need to get our eyes off ourselves and on the needs of others. This will lessen our pain even if it does not alleviate it completely.

When our affliction makes us self-oriented, it wins. But when we use it to be others-oriented, we win. We all win. If you are suffering, use it as motivation to minister to someone else.

8. *With desire for a mediator—Job 9:33*

> *"If only there were someone to arbitrate between us, to lay his hand upon us both."*
> JOB 9:33

"Guess what? I'm a meditator," my oldest son proudly proclaimed one day when he came home from elementary school.

Cathy and I looked at each other. *Oh no*, we thought. *That guidance counselor at school must be teaching some bizarre New Age stuff.*

"What will you do as a meditator?" Cathy asked him.

He smiled. "I'll help kids who get in arguments at recess fix their problem and get along."

Cathy looked at me and said, "He doesn't mean *meditator*; he means *mediator*."

"That's right," he said. "I'm supposed to help kids who get in arguments at recess. I have to understand both points of view and help them get together."

What Job came to realize in his afflicted condition was that all of us need a mediator between us and our holy God. We have sinned; God is not happy. We have questions about how He is running the universe. And in one sense, He is far from us. We need a mediator, someone who can understand both points of view and bring us together.

Job was written thousands of years before Jesus came to earth. What we know now in the twenty-first century that Job did not know is that the perfect Mediator has come.

> *For there is one God and one mediator between God*
> *and men, the man Christ Jesus.*
> 1 TIMOTHY 2:5

When you are hurting, you don't need a new *explanation* about God as much as you need a new *experience* with God. You do not need more information; you need more of God. Job struggled to get to God, but we have access to the Father through the Son, Jesus (Ephesians 2:18). His life, death, burial, and resurrection are the door from your pain to God's heart.

God loves you more than you can imagine.

Take your sorrow to Him.

Allow His grace to comfort.

Be encouraged by the many blessings God can bring into your life through your suffering, especially the blessing of a closer relationship with Him.

Note

1. National Center for Health Statistics, Data Warehouse, "LCWK9: Deaths, Percent of Total Deaths, and Death Rates for the 15 Leading Causes of Death: United States and Each State, 1999–2003," http://www.cdc.gov/nchs/datawh/statab/unpubd/mortabs/lcwk9_10.htm